Sin City Advisor's
Topless Vegas

Sin City Advisor's
Topless Vegas

Arnold Snyder

HUNTINGTON PRESS
LAS VEGAS, NEVADA

Sin City Advisor's
Topless Vegas

Published by
Huntington Press
3665 Procyon Street
Las Vegas, NV 89103
Phone (702) 252-0655
e-mail: books@huntingtonpress.com

Copyright ©2009, Arnold Snyder

ISBN: 978-1-935396-29-1

Production: Laurie Shaw

Cover image: Richard Anderson/SinCityGlamour.com; MGM Mirage; Jerry Metellus
(these are for Daisy at Rick's Cabaret, Moorea Beach, and Fantasy pinup, respectively); Las Vegas
cityscape News Bureau

Inside cover and section pages: ©Dreamstime.com/Oorka
Running heads: ©Dreamstime.com/Madartists & Day908; iStockphoto.com/Julie Fisher

Interior: Richard Anderson/SinCityGlamour.com: 2, 4, 14, 26, 36, 38, 43, 61, 62, 63, 98, 99,
103, 106, 107, 172; ©iStockphoto.com: 10 (Konstantin Tavrov), 11 (Craig Honeysett), 50, 130
(Neil Sullivan), 55, 94, 138 (Anna Lubovedskaya), 75, 247 (Martin Carlsson), 83, 118 (Valentin
Casarsa), 85 (TexPhoto), 92 (Jez Gunnell), 133 (Shane Kato), 121 (Ana Blazic), 141 (Sunagatov
Dmitry), 148 (allgord), 161 (Vasko Miokovic), 227 (Jason Stitt), 229 (Dewayne Flowers), 231
(swetta), 173 (VectorZilla), 174 (imacon); Raymond Pistol: 14, 163, 164; Jerry Metellus: 28, 250,
251, 252; Seamless: 29, 111; Matt Stabile: 34, 269; Shirlee Severs: 60, 65, 68, 70, 74, 82, 84,
86, 88, 90, 93, 95, 97, 101, 108, 113, 114, 116, 119, 128, 129, 135, 142, 144, 152, 156, 159,
162; Ray Alamo: 71, 72, 78, 80, 81; Bethany Coffey: 76, 124, 126; Foreplay Enterprises: 155;
The Light Group: 167, 192; Stratosphere: 170, 200, 240, 241; Getty Images: 182, 257 (Ethan
Miller); Flamingo Las Vegas: 183; Golden Nugget Las Vegas: 185; Station Casinos: 187, 195;
MGM Mirage: 189; 190; Rio Las Vegas: 197; TAO Beach: 202, 205; Cirque du Soleil: 209 (To-
masz Rossa), 272 (Tomas Muscionico), 273 (Phillip Dixon); N9NE Group/Playboy Club: 217, 218;
Denise Truscello: 259; Platinum Productions: 261, 262, 264

for Karen
for encouraging me to keep moving
in the direction of my dreams
no matter how nutty those dreams may be

Acknowledgments

First and foremost, I must acknowledge the Catholic Church for introducing me to the wonderful world of sin at an impressionable young age—the priests of St. Jude's Parish in my hometown, Detroit, who trained me as a choirboy and an altar boy; the Dominican nuns who taught me in elementary school; the Marist Fathers who taught me in high school; the Holy Ghost Fathers in Ann Arbor, Michigan, where I attended the seminary in the ninth grade studying for the priesthood; but mostly just to the Church itself, that glorious institution that helps form young minds, I must say thanks a bunch. Without you, Holy Mother Church, this book would not have been possible.

I'd also like to thank Anthony Curtis, my publisher and friend, for believing in this project and making it happen, and Deke Castleman, the best editor in the business, and all of the amazing staff at Huntington Press—especially Jessica, Bethany, and Laurie—for their tireless devotion to turning this crazy idea into a book.

Finally, I have to thank Karen, my wife, my gambling partner, and my best friend, who edits not only my writing, but my hair, my clothes, my diet, and pretty much everything else in my life, so that people think I'm a much cooler guy than I actually am.

Contents

Introduction

If you're looking for information on the best strip clubs in Las Vegas, you just hit the jackpot, Jack. You've found the ultimate Las Vegas guide to girls peeling off their underthings in public.

Sin City has 20 strip joints where the girls dance topless, 9 clubs where they dance completely nude, 10 casino shows that feature topless dancers, and 12 adults-only topless pools. We've got stage strip shows, table dances, lap dances, couch dances, nude bed dances, oil wrestling, bikini bull-riding, naughty-schoolgirl contests, shower shows, wet T-shirt contests, Monday Night Football titty blizzards, stripper dinner dates, a modern version of stripper taxi dancing, and nightclubs with go-go dancers in sexy lingerie. Hell, there's even a club with stripper karaoke!

As a traveling man, I've been to strip clubs in just about every state in the U.S.—including Alaska and Hawaii—and a lot of other countries as well, and I've never seen another town like this one for strip clubs. The best strip clubs in Las Vegas are some of the best strip clubs in the world!

And Jack, I cover it all. I'm a man who's found his calling. I spend my every waking moment looking at naked girls so that when you get into town, no matter what you're looking for, I can steer you in the right direction. I give you 100% honest reviews of exactly what you can expect. If I like a place, I tell you why. If I don't like a place, I give it to you straight. I list the prices for everything and whether or not I think they're worth it. I also fill you in on how to avoid getting ripped off and provide tricks the locals use to have maximum fun at minimum cost.

But do you really need a guide to strip clubs?

Yes, Jack, more than you think. All strip clubs are not created equal, and this is especially true in a town like Vegas, where there are so many clubs to choose from. How many? Here's an example. With an estimated 10,000 strippers living in Las Vegas, g-string superstores are open seven days a week. Not only are there nearly 30 topless and nude clubs worthy of inclusion in this book, but scores more massage parlors, "sex-tease" establishments, swingers clubs, porn shops with peepholes and the like, along with hundreds of "dating" or escort services, can tempt the unwary or uninformed visitor. If it's not in *Topless Vegas*, my advice is to steer clear.

Some of the girls of Badda Bing

2

Here's another example of how you can profit from the information in this book. Did you know that Las Vegas taxicab drivers get paid a kickback for every guy they deliver, even from some of the low-end dives? Consequently, a cabbie's definition of the "best strip club in town" is simply the one that puts the most dollars into his pocket. It has nothing to do with the quality of the entertainment inside.

If you tell a cabbie which club you want to go to, insist that he take you *there*. Cabbies will attempt to dissuade you from clubs that pay a lower "spiff" (this term and others of the stripper trade are defined in the Glossary, starting on pg. 305) by telling you that the club you want to go to is a gay hangout or has all old and ugly dancers, in order to drop you off at a club that pays them more. The differences in what cabbies get from the clubs are significant, ranging from $20 up to more than $100 per head, so you can't blame them for trying. Bottom line: Once you hit the Vegas turf, there really are no reliable sources for strip club information.

Or maybe you're a tourist who already knows which club you want to go to, but you take a cab instead of your rental car, because you don't know the town and you don't want to get lost. Savvy move, right? Not necessarily. Because, if you arrive at a strip club in a taxi, you're often charged a higher admission fee than a guy who comes in his own vehicle. Many of the clubs in Vegas charge a cover (as high as $30) for out-of-towners, but locals get in for less—and often free. How is this policy enforced? Arrive at the entrance in a cab and pay up. Simple as that.

How do you handle this? Here's how. When you walk up to the window, even if you didn't arrive in a cab, the cashier usually just says, "Thirty dollars." Tourists (and some locals!) don't know that if they

When you're trying to get into a club that allows locals in for free and your driver's license is from another state, all you have to do is say, "I'm a local," or "I live here," and the cashier will usually smile and let you in.

3

answer, "I'm a local," or "I live here," the cashier will usually smile and say, "Go right in."

At some clubs, you're asked to show your ID. Does that mean the jig is up? Not usually. Just because you don't have a Nevada driver's license with a Las Vegas address on it *doesn't mean you're not a local*. Not in this town. Thousands of Las Vegas residents have out-of-state licenses. People are moving here constantly. So when you're trying to get into a club that allows locals in for free and your driver's license is from another state, all you have to do is say something like, "I just moved here two weeks ago and haven't changed my license yet." Again, that won't work if a cab just dropped you off. Believe me, if the club paid a cabbie a head fee for delivering you and your ID is from out of state, *you're gonna pay the cover*.

Have I saved you this book's cost yet? You won't find this kind of information in any other guidebook, or online, or anywhere else but here. Just the facts, Jack, just the facts.

How I Went from Blackjack to Lap Dances

It's not easy to become an expert at watching women take their clothes off. For 30 years, I've been a professional gambler and gambling writer, providing accurate advice to players on how to make money playing blackjack, poker tournaments, and hustling Internet ca-

A scene from Sapphire

sino bonuses—how-to books on getting by in this world without doing anything so drastic as actually getting a job.

With this book, I'm charting new territory. Because it was important to both my publisher and me that *Topless Vegas* provide the impartial truth, free from the influence of freebies or kickbacks, my publisher paid my way into the strip joints, bought all my drinks, provided me with tip money for the dancers, treated me to dinner in the more elegant clubs that have gourmet restaurants, and required me to visit every strip joint in town on his dime, so that I could get the story from the customers' perspective. I had to visit each club as a customer, without notifying club personnel in advance that I was a reporter coming to review their establishment. And as we intend to keep this information updated on a regular basis, I now have an expense account that allows me to continue spending a hell of a lot of my free time watching women disrobe and dance around naked, while my gambling buddies are in the same strip clubs blowing their bankrolls. Eat your hearts out, you jealous bastards!

For some years now, when people I've just met ask me what I do for a living, I've enjoyed answering, "I play cards." But now, it's even better. When asked what I do, I can answer, "I watch women take their clothes off."

Hey, don't look at me like that, Jack. I'm a professional! It's a tough job, but someone's got to do it.

What You Won't Find in This Book

This guidebook is about legal entertainment, not getting laid (whether legally or illegally). Everything I cover between these two covers is legal and moral—a bona fide Las Vegas flesh fantasy. Real-live sex is beyond the scope of this book, but here's what you're looking at, Jack, when it comes to the down and dirty.

No matter what you look like, if you're a guy who's at least a bit familiar with the rules of attraction and the game of seduction, Vegas happens to be a town where it's not all that difficult to get sex if you prowl the bars and nightclubs looking for a willing partner. People come here to let loose and have fun, and as many female as male tourists are here to drink, gamble, and party.

If you're not into playing the pick-up game, legal brothels are located in Pahrump, about 60 miles west of Las Vegas. But this isn't a brothel guide, either. I'm strongly in favor of legal prostitution and I fully agree with our illustrious mayor, Oscar Goodman, that Las Vegas should have a legal red-light district downtown. But I don't review the out-of-town brothels, because I don't see any meaningful way to compare the blowjobs at the Cherry Patch to those at the Chicken Ranch. If that's what you're looking for, you'll just have to sample the women in those places yourself.

Most brothels provide free limo rides to and from Las Vegas if you call them. If you're staying in a hotel, ask the concierge or any bellman for the names of them. And don't feel sheepish about soliciting this kind of information. This is Vegas, Jack, not Salt Lake City. Brothels are legal establishments in Nevada, licensed by the state, and concierges have been arranging limos to these joints since Vegas was a two-bit cowboy town. You can also ask any cab driver and he'll be happy to take you on an hour's drive to a legal whorehouse (cabbies get a big kickback from these joints too). If you've got your own car, just head west on Highway 160 (Blue Diamond Road), which intersects the south end of the Strip about five miles south of Tropicana Avenue and takes you right into Pahrump, where you'll see billboards advertising the local whorehouses.

Prostitution, however, is illegal in Clark County—where Las Vegas is located—so be very careful about hiring "escorts" or going to massage parlors in Vegas, as you may not get what you're looking for and you can't exactly complain to the cops or the Better Business Bureau if you think you've been ripped off. The Las Vegas Yellow Pages has hundreds of suggestive ads for massage parlors and "entertainers," ads with titles like "College Girls in Short Skirts," "Barely Legal Asian Teenagers," and "Naughty Nurses"—all promising "full service," as if that means anything. A gas station down the street from my house also offers "full service," but I doubt the service-station attendant will give you a hummer after he changes your oil.

My advice: Go to Pahrump where it's legal, the women are examined weekly for VD, condoms are required for all services, and no scam artists take advantage of tourists who have no legal recourse and would likely be too embarrassed to complain if ripped off anyway. If you go to a legal whorehouse, you'll get exactly what you pay for and you won't go home with crabs, herpes, or AIDS.

You'll also see "porno slappers" who work in heavily trafficked areas along the Strip and downtown—men and women passing out business-card-sized ads or cheap pulp booklets with nude photos and phone numbers of "entertainers" you can have sent to your room. With STDs rampant in this country, why take a chance on an encounter with a woman whose phone number you got from a recent parolee out on the street? What's your plan if the cute "entertainer" you called shows up at your hotel room, takes your money, and walks out?

Other places I don't cover in this guide are the little strip-mall storefronts on Industrial Road and a few other streets off the beaten path, with signs outside that say "Hot Girls" or "Nude Girls" or "Exotic Entertainment" or something like that. These places are essentially the same as most of the massage parlors, in that what they offer is just a small private room where you can go with a girl for a price. The prices are high and, again, there are no guarantees. I've heard many stories through the years of men being ripped off in these es-

> "Prostitution is illegal in Las Vegas, so be careful about hiring "escorts" or going to massage parlors in Vegas. You can't exactly complain to the cops if you've been ripped off."

tablishments. In all cases the customers expected sex and paid a lot of money for nothing. And don't think you'll get your thousand bucks refunded if you're not satisfied with the services rendered. These joints all have big scary bouncers on the premises who are there to make sure no customer "causes trouble."

By the same token, you should never go to a strip club expecting to get laid. I won't bullshit you and state that acts of prostitution never occur in strip clubs. In fact, I've been propositioned myself by dancers in strip clubs. This is a loose town and money talks. But by and large, most strippers aren't prostitutes, and if you're looking to get laid, strip clubs aren't your ticket. A stripper doesn't want to have an affair with you. She won't pass on a venereal disease and you won't get her pregnant. She's not about to fall in love with you or call you at home and make trouble with your wife or girlfriend. She's not going to have a pimp waiting outside to beat you up and rob you. And the cops will never arrest you in a prostitution sting. Going to strip clubs is 100% legal and the dancers are there to make money legally by providing a show.

For Those Who Find the Contents of This Book Shocking ...

This is an honest, blunt, and profane guide to adult entertainment, and it's inevitable that it'll fall into the hands of some people who will be shocked by its contents. They'll probably feel that Las Vegas truly deserves its nickname, "Sin City," and that no place on Earth could be as evil and as filled with debauchery.

In fact, every big city in every state has "gentlemen's clubs." Some cities have even more than Las Vegas. And while Vegas may be pushing the boundaries of creativity in strip-club entertainment, it's no secret that lap dancing, VIP rooms, and private shows have been around for decades. It's a scene that many—if not most—men know intimately, but few ever talk about with women or anyone who would be shocked by it.

There are about 3,600 strip clubs in the U.S. and the top clubs, many of which are publicly traded on one stock exchange or another, are valued at between $700 million and $1 billion. It's impossible to put a number on how many American women work as dancers in strip clubs, but it's somewhere in the hundreds of thousands. The strip-club industry provides some of the highest paying jobs available to women who don't have advanced degrees. In Jack Sheehan's well-researched *Skin City: Uncovering the Las Vegas Sex Industry* (Stephens Press, 2004), the author estimates that there could be as many as 15,000 strippers in Las Vegas, based on the number of sheriff's cards (work permits) issued in Clark County for exotic dancers. He also states that the average income for a full-time Vegas dancer—working at least four nights a week—is between $85,000 and $250,000.

No business could possibly grow this big without catering to a basic human need for a large portion of the population. In the countries where strip clubs don't exist, the women are second-class citizens and the men are repressed by religious and moral codes enforced via threats of imprisonment or worse.

If you're a guy who's never been to a strip club, I highly recommend this pastime as a rewarding hobby that's guaranteed to brighten up your outlook on life. When you come out of a strip club, you always feel good—the same way you feel when you come out of an art gallery or a nature conservatory. To spend a few hours just appreciating beauty is one of the most emotionally healthy things you can do. When you go to a strip club, you're rewarding yourself just for being alive and having a robust sensory relationship with the world around you.

On any given night, Las Vegas is home base
for as many as 15,000 strippers.

How to Use This Guide

The rest of this book is organized into three parts: Strip Clubs, Topless Pools, and Nightclubs and Casino Shows. The reviews within each part are arranged alphabetically.

You'll also find introductory material in the beginning of each part. Part One—The Strip Clubs, for example, includes chapters on strip-club etiquette, tipping procedures, and the law regarding strip-club behavior. These all differ from state to state and city to city, so even if you frequent strip clubs in your hometown, you should read these sections to see how it all works in Las Vegas. In Part Two—Topless Pools, you'll find an explanation of the difference between American-style and European-style pools.

As for the reviews themselves, although they're based on my own ongoing experience and research, strip clubs do occasionally change ownership, as well as policies and prices. I'll do my best to update the information in this book as I learn of changes. Also, some of the information herein was provided to me by dancers, bartenders, or other club employees, and sometimes these people make mistakes. For example, very few strip clubs post lap-dance or VIP-room prices and on more than one occasion, I was provided with erroneous information by the first person I talked with. If you find any errors or omissions, or you have any comments, criticisms, or arguments with any of what's included in this book, please contact me so that I can correct it. If you're a club manager, dancer, or other employee of a strip club, contact me if you know of any special events, weekly contests, or other happenings at your club, and I'll make sure they get posted (and reviewed) on http://SinCityAdvisor.com. You can also email me directly at: arnoldsnyder@live.com.

Part One

The Strip Clubs

1

Topless vs Nude

To drink or not to drink, that is the question.

To see pussy or not to see pussy, that is the answer!

The Las Vegas municipal code allows establishments that serve liquor to feature topless, but not bottomless, dancers. If an establishment serves soft drinks only, the dancers can take it all off. Apparently, the city lawmakers came to the conclusion that if a man is drinking alcohol, he cannot handle looking at pussy. If he's drinking Pepsi, then pussy's fine. God only knows what kind of atrocities might be committed by a man under the simultaneous influence of beer and pussy.

To be sure, this particular bit of regulation affects a lot more than just whether or not you're going to see female genitalia in a Las Vegas strip club. The overall quality of the stage shows, the age and talent of the dancers, and the amount of physical contact you can expect during lap dances and VIP-room shows are all essentially determined by this beer-for-pussy trade-off. As a general rule, the topless clubs are about drinking, lap dancing, and darkness, while the nude clubs are about younger dancers and better stage shows.

Where are they? The clubs are scattered across the valley, with the greatest concentration around Sahara Ave., west of I-15. See the map of locations on pg. 39.

Topless Clubs

All the topless clubs in Las Vegas serve alcohol, so you must be 21 to enter. Young guys should expect to get carded. If you look young and don't have a photo ID to prove your age, don't waste your time trying to get in. The same age restriction applies to the dancers: If alcohol is served at a club, a dancer must be 21 to work there.

Most of the topless clubs aren't so much strip clubs as lap-dance clubs. They tend to be dark, with lots of comfortable chairs and loud music. All have VIP areas or booths in rooms where a dancer can entertain you more privately for a higher charge. Because they focus on lap dances, most topless clubs in Las Vegas have small poorly lit main stages where dancers have little room to move—as a rule, the bigger the club, the smaller the stage(s) and the less emphasis given the stage show. (I point out the few topless clubs with better stage shows in my reviews.)

Most topless clubs have a cover charge of $10 to $30 for non-locals, while locals can usually get in for free by flashing a Nevada driver's license. A beer rarely costs less than $5 to $6 in a topless joint (except during happy

Both topless and nude clubs offer lap dances and/or VIP rooms, but you'll generally get a lot more physical contact for your buck in the topless joints, such as Sapphire, pictured here.

hours), and in some clubs a domestic beer runs more than $10. A few topless clubs have drink specials for locals—again, see my reviews.

Many topless clubs, because they have full bars, are open 24/7. This doesn't mean you'll find dancers at all hours of the day and night. The busiest times are from about 11 p.m. to 4 a.m. If you go to a topless club at 10 a.m., or 2 p.m., you may find no dancers at all, or just one or two hanging around to see if any of the guys who come into the club for a drink want to go to the VIP room. Also, the dancers who tend to be available in these off-hours are often on the lower-end of the talent/beauty scale. The top earners generally get assigned to the most lucrative shifts.

The silicone factor in the Las Vegas topless clubs is high, with big breasts the norm in the most popular clubs. If you're a tit man, the topless clubs will appeal to you much more than the nude clubs.

Both topless and nude clubs offer lap dances and/or VIP rooms, but you'll generally get a lot more physical contact for your buck in the topless joints. This may be because the dancers in the topless clubs are older and have been around the scene longer, or simply because it's the only way they make money. Stage dancers in the topless clubs make far less in tips than stage dancers in the nude clubs, so lap dances and VIP-room shows are their main source of income.

The most common price for a lap dance in a topless club is $20 and it lasts for one song (about three minutes). The most common

> "The silicone factor in the Las Vegas topless clubs is high, with big breasts the norm in the most popular clubs. If you're a tit man, the topless clubs will appeal to you much more than the nude clubs."

minimum price for the VIP room in a topless club is $100 for three songs, or about nine to ten minutes with the dancer. You might wonder why three lap dances in the main room cost you $60, while in the VIP room it's $100. The answer is that the VIP room provides more privacy and in most cases, the dancers allow and encourage more physical contact. Many dancers, for example, don't allow customers to touch their breasts out on the main floor, but do allow it in the VIP.

Most topless clubs require VIP-room customers to pay for a dancer's time and incur a bar tab. In most cases, this tab is entirely separate from any you may have already incurred in the club. For example, you purchase a drink for yourself and a dancer just before you enter the VIP room, drinks in hand. If the VIP room requires a bar tab, those drinks don't count. Many dancers neglect to tell you that the VIP room also requires a bar tab, so before going in with a dancer, ask if a bar tab is required and how much. Also, don't be surprised if the required drinks in the VIP room cost more than in the main room.

Most dancers are ethical and don't try to extort more money than a customer has agreed in advance to pay. Some, however, are not. If you spring for $200 for a half-hour, a dancer might try to tell you at the end of your time in the VIP that you that need to pay an extra $100, because you went 10 or 15 minutes over the time limit. The easiest way to keep out of this predicament is to make the deal clear before you enter the room, asking her to let you know when the agreed-upon time is up. The other way to keep out of this type of trouble is to look at your watch when your VIP time starts, tell her what time it is, then pay attention to the time so that you don't go over. Again, with most dancers, none of this is necessary. They'll pay attention. In some clubs, the bouncer or a VIP waitress keeps track of the time and informs you when it's up. But there are definitely a few scammers in this business.

VIP rooms in the topless clubs tend to be multi-customer rooms with open booths, where anywhere from five to a dozen or more dancers may be entertaining customers simultaneously. What you can expect from a dancer in a VIP room with regards to physical contact is often a function of how much you tip and how gentle you are, in addition to the dancer's personal standards. Most don't allow a customer to touch their genitals and you shouldn't expect a dancer in a topless club to get naked for you, a violation of the law in an establishment that serves liquor.

How do you find out what a dancer will allow in the VIP? There are many ways.

First, pay attention to her approach when she comes on to you. If she starts nuzzling into your neck while saying something like, "C'Mon, baby, let's go get naughty," then sits down in your lap, slips her hand inside your shirt, and starts caressing your nipples and squirming around, that's a sign that she's into physical contact. Dancers who come on strong usually mean it. If she stands apart from you, on the other hand, and says something like, "Do you want a dance?" that tends to be a sign that she's not going to encourage, and may even discourage, a lot of physical contact. This may seem obvious, but many men are pretty dense about body language. They choose girls for lap dances who look like their "type"—buxom, blonde, Latino, or whatever—and then they're disappointed when they don't get the treatment they were hoping for.

Guys looking for high-mileage VIP-room dances should try out a lap dance on the main floor first, giving it what one of my buddies calls "the titty test." She sits in your lap and starts grinding. You reach for titty. She blocks access and says something like, "Not out here." Bingo! She's telling you that things are different in the VIP. On the other hand, if she just blocks access and says nothing, or says something like, "Keep your hands down,"

Key Numbers

These fluctuate, but you can expect to pay approximately these rates in a topless club.

Cover charge... $10-$30
Beer................ $6+
Lap dance $20
VIP room......... $100
(3 dances)

17

you should understand that you won't be getting to second base with this girl.

Also, before you commit to going into the VIP, you can always ask a dancer exactly what you're allowed to do in there. Some dancers will respond pretty straightforward to this question. "You can touch me on top but not between my legs." If you go this direct route, don't be crude. Dancers don't like guys who are rough or disrespectful. Start by complimenting her. Tell her she has the most beautiful breasts you've ever seen and that she's gorgeous and you love the way she danced on stage. If you open with compliments, then ask politely if she'll allow you to touch her breasts in the VIP room, you'll more likely get a positive response.

Nude Clubs

If a strip club doesn't serve alcohol, the minimum age for dancers and customers is 18 and the girls can dance nude. (If you look anywhere near 18, you'll definitely be carded, so always carry your ID.) The good news for guys under 21, however, is that you get to see pussy and the stage shows are way sexier than any of those you'll ever see in the topless clubs.

Even if you're 21 or older, you're better off heading to the nude clubs if you really like watching, as opposed to having physical contact with, dancers, assuming you can go without alcohol. The stages in the nude clubs tend to be bigger and better lit, and the dancers have more room to move.

If you want a good stage show and booze, a few topless clubs have better shows than others and I mention these in my reviews. There's also one nude club in North Las Vegas, the Palomino Club, where alcohol is served. (As Las Vegas' oldest strip club still in operation, the Palomino's special status was grandfathered, as the club had nude dancing before the municipal code was changed to disallow it in drinking establishments.) The Palomino is reviewed in the Nude Clubs chapter.

Topless vs Nude

Nude clubs, despite their cover charges, tend to be less expensive than topless clubs overall: The soft drinks are often provided at no charge. In addition, there's no bar-tab requirement in the VIP rooms.

Because they don't have full bars, nude clubs aren't open round the clock. Some open in the early afternoon, but more commonly in the early evening. The busy times are earlier than in the topless clubs—generally from about 9 p.m. to 2 a.m.—probably because they cater to a younger and more sober clientele. As in the topless clubs, you'll find

The stage shows in nude clubs like Talk of the Town (pictured) are much sexier than in the topless joints, and nude clubs tend to be less expensive overall.

that the quality of the dancers goes up during the busy hours.

Many dancers in the nude clubs have natural breasts. If your idea of sexy is an 18-year-old girl with cute (and real) little titties, you'll like the nude clubs a lot better than the topless clubs. And obviously, if your idea of sexy is seeing a dancer's pussy, nude clubs are the way to go. Don't be surprised if you see some radical body adornment in the way of piercings and tattoos, and I'm not talking about the "normal" tattoos and piercings that have become so popular in the past decade or so. I'm talking about major works of skin art.

Again, the nude clubs tend to have big well-lit stages and the dancers at the best ones are experts at working the poles and the crowd. Their floor shows are highly erotic and they spend a lot of time entertaining guys on the rail who are tipping.

One important difference between the nude and topless clubs is that the girls in the nude clubs, many of whom are younger, are generally a lot stingier with physical contact in the VIP rooms. A dancer here is more likely to limit the amount and areas of touching and some may tell you up front that touching costs extra or is simply not allowed. Why? Some of the girls are younger and they feel more vulnerable. VIP rooms in the nude clubs tend to be one-on-one private rooms or cubicles, not big open areas with lots of other dancers and customers around. Also, usually no bouncer is there to watch the action (though one is always close by). And again, the girls are completely naked, not even wearing a g-string.

Some of the nude clubs, like Little Darlings, definitely try to cater to men who prefer younger-looking girls, as evidenced by the name of the club and some of their promotions, such as the "Naughty Schoolgirl Contest." The nude clubs also tend to attract real dancers who prefer performing on stage over the high degrees of physical contact in the topless clubs. Although many of these dancers are under 21, quite a few are in their mid-20s and even 30s who tend to look younger than

Some of the nude clubs definitely try to cater to men who prefer younger-looking girls.

they are, simply because trained dancers keep their bodies in excellent shape. Also, fewer dancers in the nude clubs get boob jobs, and small breasts generally look younger than large ones.

Similarly, although the crowd in the nude clubs tends to be younger, this doesn't mean that no men over 21 are in the audience. Quite a few older men who could go to the topless clubs prefer the nude clubs for a variety of reasons. They like watching the better stage shows. They prefer to see completely naked dancers. They prefer natural to surgically enhanced breasts. They don't really care that much for drinking. And their erotic orientation is more visual than tactile. Some guys simply prefer a striptease to a lap dance.

Itemizing the Differences

There are eight major differences between the nude clubs and the topless clubs:

	TOPLESS CLUBS	NUDE CLUBS
1. Alcohol served	yes	no
2. Age of dancers	older (min. age 21)	younger (min. age 18)
3. Tits	big (lots of silicone)	little (mostly natural)
4. Pussy	no	yes
5. Stage show	dark, mediocre	well-lit, excellent
6. Physical contact	high-mileage	lower-mileage
7. Locals cover charge	locals free	locals pay
8. Age of customers	all 21 or older	lots of guys 18-20

There are exceptions to some of these differences in various clubs, and I discuss these exceptions in my reviews.

2

Strip Club Etiquette

Etiquette for Customers

The following information should be obvious to any guy with half a brain, but I've heard so many dancers complain about so many customers through the years that I have to be frank. If you don't know this stuff already, read it and consider yourself educated. If you do, read it and consider yourself reminded.

1) Before you go to a strip club, take a shower, put on clean clothes, and use mouthwash and deodorant. If this doesn't make sense to you, consider it from the dancer's perspective. Imagine that it's your job to walk around a dark crowded room in a g-string, sitting in strangers' laps and hoping they don't try to pinch your nipples. Obviously, very few guys would actually have the guts to do what these women do for a living, but just try to imagine that's your job. Wouldn't you at least want these strangers to be clean?

2) If you're sitting on the rail, you should tip each dancer. If you're too broke to tip a buck, then sit somewhere else so a tipper can take your seat. This is especially true if all the other seats on the rail are occupied. The dancers you're watching are paying for the right to be there, hoping you'll think they're sexy and pretty enough to tip them. They're paid nothing by the clubs and earn their living from tips. Get a clue.

3) If a dancer approaches you to offer a lap dance, a private show, or whatever, and you have no intention of taking her up on the offer, always be polite to her. Don't cut her off when she's talking. Tell her she's cute and you're tempted, but you just want to watch the show. If she persists, just keep saying "Maybe later." Never be rude. And if you're broke, tell her you're broke.

4) Never ask a dancer for her phone number. Never ask a dancer for a date. Never ask her what her real name is. If she wants you to know what her real name is (highly unlikely), she'll tell you. If you ask her, she'll think you're a jerk. Lots of guys ask dancers for their real names, so they tend to think of lots of guys as jerks.

Even if a dancer does tell you her "real" name, it's probably just another fake name anyway. The key to what's going on here is that she's a performer. You're the audience. She's a skilled professional trying to create a fantasy world where you can pretend for the moment that she's interested in you, she finds you attractive, and you really turn her on. But you don't turn her on, so don't kid yourself. She's not thinking of you as some guy she wants to get to know. If she asks you what your name is, it's part of her act. I'm sure some naïve young dancers think they're looking for relationships with the guys they meet in the strip clubs where they work, but by and large, a dancer really doesn't care what your name is. She's doing a job and putting on a show for you and that's plenty worth the money you're paying her. When you go into a strip club, you leave the real world behind. This is fantasy land. You're here to have fun and to take away some visuals and memories, not get involved in a relationship.

Of course, some might think this to be naïve. When I say, "Never ask a dancer for her phone number," or for a date or what her real name is, I know there's no such thing as *never*. Dancers are human and they're sometimes attracted to guys in the clubs where they work. Employees of the club—bartenders, bouncers, hosts, managers—have more of a shot at developing a relationship with a dancer than a customer does because they're part of the scene. They have time to get to know dancers on a more personal level. But if you're a local and hang out at Cheetahs or Rick's seven nights a week, 364 nights a year (you go to Mass on Christmas Eve), you may get involved in the lives of at least some of the dancers, and one of them might wind up as your girl-friend, or even your wife. Chemistry works in mysterious ways.

Sometimes, dancers are attracted to customers who simply fit their "type." Dancers who are socially rebellious might be attracted to guys who strike them the same way—outlaw bikers, musicians in rock bands, natural "bad boys," etc. Guys who work in glamour pro-fessions—acting, athletics, or any type of entertainment-industry job, which in Vegas might be a stand-up comic, a magician, a singer, etc.— are more likely to get a dancer's phone number than a working stiff in some mundane dead-end job.

And some guys are just good at picking up girls. They're funny and charming and flirty and confident—and it's not that they're skilled at scoring with dancers so much as scoring with women, period. But most of these guys would probably find it easier to hook up with a date in a pick-up bar than in a strip club, because most dancers really are there to work and make money and many aren't open to having social relationships with customers.

Oh yes, and millionaires who are dripping hundred-dollar bills as they walk might also find it easier than most guys to pick up a dancer, but then these dudes also find it easier to pick up secretaries, wait-resses, college girls, and anything else wearing a skirt, and that's just the world we live in.

But those situations happen to, perhaps, 1% of the guys who visit Las Vegas strip clubs. The other 99% of us are just there for a flesh fantasy and shouldn't consider making a play for one of the dancers. In this book, I'm addressing the 99% of you. The other 1% don't need me to tell them anything (though they might learn a little something about titty ball in the Topless Pool chapter).

5) If you're with a dancer who allows you to fondle or caress her during a lap or VIP-room dance, never try to touch her in any way that she discourages. She should not have to discourage your hands more than once. And always touch her gently. If she lets you feel her up, never squeeze or pinch her nipples. Never be rough in any way, and never, ever, try to kiss a dancer on the mouth. Respect every dancer's

limits, even when she's driving you to the brink of your self-control. Remember, it's not what the club allows or what the law allows, it's what the dancer allows, and if you try to violate her limits, don't be surprised if she disappears as soon as she can.

What if every guy in the VIP room is getting a full-contact lap dance, while the dancer with you is into air dancing only? Live with it! Treat her with respect. If you feel what you're getting is far below the normal standards for this club and you've seen this dancer provide full-contact laps for other guys, then I'd suggest you go back and reread Etiquette Rule #1.

The central theme to these rules of etiquette is this: Always show respect for the dancers. If you're under the impression that dancing in a strip club is an easy lifestyle, you're mistaken. I've heard guys say that in their opinion, dancers just get "money for nothing." In fact,

stage performance is always stressful and difficult, even for those who are born exhibitionists and thrive on the rush of performing. Many stage actors and singers get physically sick before performances. Musicians, stand-up comics, and public speakers have long used alcohol and drugs just to do what they do on stage. Strippers are no different. As with rock and jazz musicians, stand-up comics, and all nightclub performers, the competition for jobs is fierce,

Ultimately, the dancer dictates the level of contact during a lap dance.

the lifestyle invites exploitation of the artists by club personnel, and the loose party environment makes access to drugs and alcohol easy and abuse widespread. In the same sense that we show respect for the bands that get us revved up and the comics who make us laugh, we should respect strippers for giving us fantasies, making us smile, and turning us on.

Oh, yes, one other rule …

6) Don't fart in the VIP room.

Tipping Etiquette

Las Vegas strip-club dancers work for tips. They're not employees of the clubs where they work. Like the customers, they pay to get in the door, and they pay the club more to work there than the customers pay to see them work. Depending on the club, stage fees and tipouts can cost each dancer upwards of $100 per shift. If a dancer doesn't garner substantially more than her club fees in tips, she cannot afford to work as a dancer.

Stiffing dancers you like is therefore a greater sin than not tipping waitresses in restaurants. Waitresses, at least, don't pay to work. The only reason you go to a strip club is to see the dancers. No one goes to a strip club, where the drinks are so overpriced, just to have a beer. Besides, these clubs have little else to offer.

One of the reasons we see so many unattractive and talentless dancers is that the standards are low. If a dancer can generate enough tip money to survive, the club has nothing to lose by keeping her on. Some terrible dancers are good at hustling tips. Some of the best dancers aren't all that skilled as hustlers.

As a general rule, you should tip the dancers you like the most and don't tip the dancers you don't care for. If I don't like most of the dancers in a club, I don't patronize that club. If I don't care for a particular dancer on stage, I get off the rail. I view a lap dance primarily as a way to tip a dancer I really like. A lot of guys view a lap dance as a way to feel up a dancer who has big tits, and for this reason a lot of less-than-stellar dancers make a lot of money.

Be prepared to tip or face the consequences.

Every club has a set fee for a lap dance—usually $20, though a few clubs charge $30 and one charges only $10. You can ask any dancer what a lap dance costs and they'll all quote the fee set by the house. You never have to tip a lap dancer more than this amount for a lap dance. But if you give the dancer an extra $5 or $10, she really appreciates it. If you don't have the money for a lap dance and you really like a dancer, tip her $5 or whatever you can afford when she comes around trying to sell laps. Tell her you want to tip her because you dig the way she dances, but you don't have the money for a lap dance.

Remember that the dancers make their money from us, not the clubs, and we want to ensure the survival of the finest. And don't forget that dancers are performers. Applause is often as important to a performer as money, and there's very little applause for stage dancers in strip clubs. If you get a lap dance, lavish the dancer with praise for her beauty, her talent, her sexiness. These women work hard for their money, so say whatever you can to let the really good dancers know how much they're appreciated.

The Bouncer

Usually, a bouncer stands at the entryway to the VIP room. It's his job to make sure there are no problems. You're not a stiff if you don't tip the bouncer. But it might not be a bad idea to take care of him on your way in if you're hoping for a high-mileage dance and you want as much privacy as you can get. He may be able to steer other VIP room arrivals away from you. Toke him $10 for the minimal time allotment (usually three songs) or $20 for a half-hour or more.

Sometimes a dancer will ask you to tip the bouncer or to give her some money to tip the bouncer. The dancers must tip the bouncers as part of their tipout, so if you like the dancer and she treats you well, contributing to the bouncer is considered the gentlemanly thing to do. If you're on a strict budget, however, and you've just spent your rent money on the VIP room, the bar tab, and a little extra for the dancer, if she asks you to contribute to the bouncer's tip, politely tell her you're tapped out.

3

Strip Club Particulars

Can you touch? Can they? The law has a lot to do with how you're expected to conduct yourself in a Las Vegas strip club. The first part of this chapter is devoted to breaking down the legalities and clearing up a few related particulars. Then I fill you in on all the details about cameras in the VIP rooms, rules for women customers, and getting to and from your car and the clubs safely. Finally, the map at the end of the chapter identifies the locations of every strip club in Las Vegas.

Strip Club Law: What's Allowed

Can a dancer be busted for pushing her tits in your face? Can she legally dry-hump you? Can you go to jail for feeling her up? Inquiring minds want to know! And believe it or not, the answers to these burning questions of our time have come all the way from the Nevada Supreme Court. Generally, I find legal arguments and court decisions about as exciting as sweeping out my garage, but these battles have been so amusing, with legal arguments so inane, that I'm compelled to fill you in on the juicy details.

The legal status of lap dancing in the city of Las Vegas goes back to a case that began in 2004, when 13 Crazy Horse Too dancers were busted for violating the Las Vegas Erotic Dance Code, which states: "No dancer shall fondle or caress any patron, and no patron shall fondle or caress any dancer."

Now, the wording of that section of the law may sound pretty clear, but no one had ever tried to enforce the Las Vegas Erotic Dance Code, since lap dancing had become common in the Las Vegas strip clubs. According to Deputy City Attorney Edward Poleski, the Las Vegas law was modeled on a decades-old decision in a Washington state case, at a time when dancers in that state were not allowed to get within 10 feet of customers and tipping was prohibited. But with no one making any effort to enforce this law in Las Vegas for so many years, "fondling and caressing" had become an established part of the strip-club scene. Then suddenly, for whatever reason, the Las Vegas District Attorney got a wild hair up his ass about it.

But before we go any further in the Crazy Horse Too case, let me tell you about some of Nevada's other stupid laws that are never enforced. Mothers in Nevada have to get licensed as cosmetologists if they want to give their own daughters a perm. Bar owners are not allowed to sell beer unless they're also cooking soup. You can be arrested if you bring a belching kid into a church. I'm not making this stuff up. You can go look up all of these laws online—like the anti-fondling provision of the strip club law, they're all real state statutes, even though, to the best of my knowledge, nobody's been trying to hassle Las Vegas mothers for giving perms.

Anyway, the Crazy Horse Too dancers fought the charges against them on the grounds that the law was "vague," since the terms fondling and caressing weren't precisely defined. And as was widely expected, the dancers won their case. It was thrown out of court by Municipal Court Judge Betsy Kolkoski, who agreed that the law was unconstitutionally vague. That should have been the end of it.

But no. The moronic city attorneys decided to appeal the case in District Court, arguing that a dancer touching a strip club patron should be deemed illegal when said dancer engages in this contact for the purpose of sexually arousing said patron. What kills me is that no one who was actually involved in this activity was complaining. No customers claimed that the dancers were offending them with their lewd behavior. No dancers asserted customers were taking advantage of them. No strip club managers called the cops to have their dancers or customers arrested. Just one stuffed shirt, Edward Poleski, in the D.A.'s office, was morally outraged that somebody out there was having more fun than he was, and he unearthed a law on the books that he felt he could use to put a stop to it!

To the dismay of the city attorneys, however, the Municipal Court judge's decision was upheld by District Judge Sally Loehrer. Judge Loehrer pointed out that since the law didn't even specify if the caressing had to be done with the hands, a dancer might be found in violation of the law if she used a feather boa to caress a customer. Judge Loehrer found the appellants' argument about sexual arousal to be particularly ridiculous. She was quoted in the *Las Vegas Sun* as stating: "Why else would anyone go into those establishments? They're not going for the lighting or the drinks. If people go in there, I would assume they are going in to be erotically aroused."

So, hallefuckinglujiah, there's actually intelligent life within the court system! It took two female judges to recognize, and be brave enough to state for the record, that guys go to strip clubs to get turned on and that the anti-fondling and caressing laws were more about harassment than protecting public morals.

But was that the end of it? Oh no. The Las Vegas city attorneys, who apparently had enough time on their hands to worry about

> " ... dancing in the Vegas topless clubs is pretty loose and the VIP room activities are even looser. ... The important point is that if she allows you to touch her, you're unlikley to be arrested for doing so and she won't be arrested for allowing you to do so. "

what strip-club patrons had on (or in) their hands, appealed the District Court's ruling to the Nevada Supreme Court. So now, the state Supreme Court was actually called upon to make a ruling on whether or not an adult woman was allowed to let a guy feel her up!

The Supreme Court Rules on Breast Fondling

In November 2006, more than two years after the alleged crime of fondling occurred at the Crazy Horse Too (which had lost its license due to tax violations and is no longer in business), the Nevada Supreme Court overturned Las Vegas District Judge Sally Loehrer's ruling and declared that the Las Vegas Erotic Dance Code was, in fact, not unconstitutionally vague! The Nevada newspapers and TV news all reported that the strippers had lost their case and that the anti-lap-dancing laws could be enforced. It looked like a dark and gloomy future for lap dances in Las Vegas.

Then someone took the time to read the full text of the Supreme Court's ruling. Although the justices had ruled that the Las Vegas law was not unconstitutionally vague (they considered the terms "fondling and caressing" sufficiently understood by the average person), they also stated in their opinion that: "Arguably, erotic dance is expressive conduct that communicates, which could be deserving of some level of First Amendment protection. If that is so, fondling and caressing may be protected expressive conduct when part of an erotic dance. Further, even if fondling and caressing as part of an erotic dance are afforded First Amendment protection as expressive conduct that communicates, the protection is not absolute. Such conduct remains subject to reasonable time, place, and manner restrictions. Therefore, to the extent that LVMC 6.35.100(I) reaches conduct arguably protected by the First Amendment, it is not overbroad so long as it is a valid time, place, and manner restriction of the arguably protected conduct that communicates, i.e., fondling and caressing as part of an erotic dance ..."

And what exactly does that mean? It means that despite the Nevada Supreme Court's finding that the Las Vegas erotic dance code was not unconstitutionally vague, none of the 13 dancers who had been busted for violating the code were brought back to court to reface the charges against them. Nor, to my knowledge, have any other strippers or strip-club customers in Las Vegas been arrested for "fondling and caressing" crimes since this Supreme Court ruling came down. The reason is that, in order to prosecute, the D.A. would have to argue that although fondling and caressing as part of an erotic-dance routine may be protected communication under the First Amendment to the Constitution, a strip-club performance is not the proper time or place for such protected activities to occur! I'd love to see the arguments in *that* case should it ever get to trial.

So What Does This Mean For Us?

It means that lap dancing in the Vegas topless clubs is pretty loose and the VIP room activities are even looser. It doesn't mean that you have a "right" to feel up any dancer who sits in your lap. The important point is that if she allows you to touch her, you're unlikely to be arrested for doing so and she won't be arrested for allowing (or even encouraging) you to do so. If she wants to exercise her First Amendment rights while she's in your lap, long live the Constitution!

If you live in Las Vegas, remember these names: Betsy Kolkoski and Sally Loehrer. When these judges are up for reelection, vote for them. Meanwhile, don't forget the name of Edward Poleski, the Deputy City Attorney who spent two years trying to have dancers convicted for violating a law that created a victimless crime. Maybe now he'll go after mothers who give their daughters perms. Should Poleski ever run for office in this town, vote for anyone but him.

Cameras in the VIP Rooms

You should also be aware that some (not all) Las Vegas strip clubs—both nude and topless—have surveillance cameras in the VIP rooms. Some have surveillance cameras in all the VIP areas. Others have cameras in some rooms, but not others. The dancers in clubs that have these cameras will tell you that their purpose is to make sure that they're not performing acts of prostitution. One club manager told me a different story, saying it was to protect the club from legal harassment in the event that a vice cop tries to bring them up on a phony prostitution charge. But prostitution busts usually stem from a dancer's verbal solicitation of an undercover vice cop for an act of prostitution. Surveillance cameras don't record sound, and since a vice cop wouldn't be allowed to actually have sex with a dancer in order to bring charges against her, this explanation makes no sense.

Many customers in the VIP rooms are unaware that they're being filmed. I suspect some would find it disturbing and many would feel that it was an invasion of privacy. Unless their main purpose is simply to discourage prostitution, I personally don't see how surveillance cameras in the VIP rooms protect the clubs at all.

The worrisome thing from the customers' perspective is not so much that some jack-off manager is watching you from his office, but that a tape of the VIP-room activities could fall into the wrong hands. If this concerns you, always ask a dancer at any club you visit if there are surveillance cameras in the VIP rooms. The dancers know and will tell you.

You can also just look for these cameras yourself. They're often housed in small dark Plexiglas half-domes on the ceiling, like casino surveillance cameras. You might also see small cylindrical lenses mounted high on a wall or the ceiling. A camera may also be mounted behind a mirror in the room.

If you don't like the idea of being filmed in the VIP, then only patronize clubs that don't use cameras. And tell the manager why you'll no longer patronize his club. If the owners see they're losing customers, they might change the club's policy.

Strip Club Particulars

Admission Policies for Women

Many Las Vegas strip clubs bar unescorted women—and by unescorted, I mean by a man. There are two main reasons for this policy. First, the strip clubs don't want prostitutes coming in and soliciting their customers, who are horny and primed for action. A strip club that tolerates independent working girls not only risks lost revenues, but could lose its license if it appeared that it was condoning the solicitation.

Second, the clubs want to avoid embarrassing scenes where angry wives or girlfriends come hunting for their men. Guys think of strip clubs as safe havens from the real world and their real lives. That's why they call them "gentlemen's clubs." They're traditionally for men only.

But as more men these days are coming into strip clubs with their wives and girlfriends, more and more clubs are allowing in unescorted women, especially when they come in groups and seem to be out on the town looking for fun. Also, young women who look like dancer material may be allowed into a club if they say they want to check out the place because they're considering auditioning there.

I had initially planned to list the clubs that do and don't allow unescorted women, but in querying doormen, cashiers, and managers, I discovered that most clubs don't have a strict policy in this regard, basing their decision to allow entry case by case.

Parking Safety

All the Las Vegas strip clubs have parking lots and many offer valet parking. Most lots are well-lit and, in my opinion, safe. Although I often use valet parking when I go to casinos, simply for the convenience of dropping my car at the entrance, I rarely use valet service at a strip joint, where all the parking lots are located adjacent to the club entrances. And even those in seedier neighborhoods or desolate warehouse districts seem safe to me.

As a six-footer who tends to walk with a swagger, I look more like someone you wouldn't want to meet in a dark alley than someone who who'd victimized in one. So I brought my wife with me on a driving tour of the strip club parking lots to get her opinion. She felt that as a woman, there were more than a few neighborhoods in which she wouldn't feel comfortable walking on the street, but she agreed that the parking lots were probably safe to use. Most are well-lit and located in view of the club entrance. Some are fenced private lots. Those that offer valet parking usually have a valet standing outside in the lot and many clubs have doormen who stand outside to greet customers. Some also have video surveillance of their lots and none tolerate vagrants or loiterers on their premises.

But—as in every other big city—crime does exist in Las Vegas, so you may opt to use valet service where I wouldn't. I list which clubs offer valet parking and which don't, with brief commentary on the lot or neighborhood where applicable, so you can decide on a case-by-case basis as you drive up to the entrance.

Rick's Cabaret has a well-lit parking lot that's patrolled by security guards.

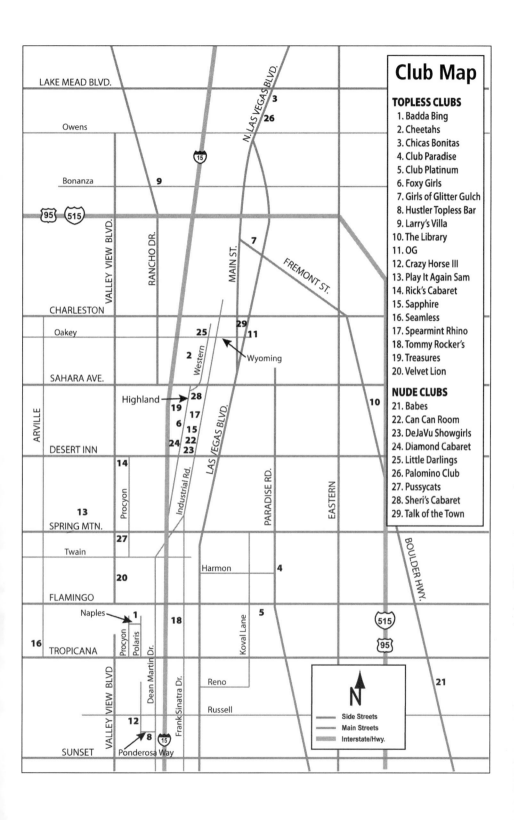

Club Map

TOPLESS CLUBS
1. Badda Bing
2. Cheetahs
3. Chicas Bonitas
4. Club Paradise
5. Club Platinum
6. Foxy Girls
7. Girls of Glitter Gulch
8. Hustler Topless Bar
9. Larry's Villa
10. The Library
11. OG
12. Crazy Horse III
13. Play It Again Sam
14. Rick's Cabaret
15. Sapphire
16. Seamless
17. Spearmint Rhino
18. Tommy Rocker's
19. Treasures
20. Velvet Lion

NUDE CLUBS
21. Babes
22. Can Can Room
23. DeJaVu Showgirls
24. Diamond Cabaret
25. Little Darlings
26. Palomino Club
27. Pussycats
28. Sheri's Cabaret
29. Talk of the Town

LAKE MEAD BLVD.
Owens
Bonanza
CHARLESTON
Oakey
SAHARA AVE.
Highland
DESERT INN
SPRING MTN.
Twain
FLAMINGO
Naples
TROPICANA
SUNSET

N. LAS VEGAS BLVD.
VALLEY VIEW BLVD.
RANCHO DR.
MAIN ST.
FREMONT ST.
Western
Wyoming
LAS VEGAS BLVD.
Industrial Rd.
PARADISE RD.
EASTERN
BOULDER HWY.
Procyon
Harmon
Koval Lane
Reno
Russell
Procyon
Polaris
Dean Martin Dr.
Frank Sinatra Dr.
Ponderosa Way
ARVILLE
VALLEY VIEW BLVD

N

Side Streets
Main Streets
Interstate/Hwy.

4

Best of The Best

As mentioned earlier, you can see strippers, all-nude dancers, topless showgirls, female nipples at pools, and the like at 50 different places in Las Vegas. That's a lot of choices, and the in-depth reviews that follow will help you decide on where to go to get what you want. If you're the impatient type, though, you won't go wrong sticking with the "best of the best," which appear in the following listings.

The first group covers the best options in several areas, including some specific to pools and shows (which are covered later in the book). The second zeroes in on your best moves for a given day of the week.

Best of the Best in Topless Clubs	
Hottest Stage Show	Rick's Cabaret Library (shower shows)
Best Lap Dance Clubs	Cheetahs Spearmint Rhino Sapphire
Plushest VIP Rooms	Badda Bing Sapphire

Best of the Best in Topless Clubs (con't)

Best VIP-Room Deal	Play It Again Sam
Most Unconventional VIP Room	Sapphire's Stripper Karaoke
Most Unconventional Concept	Seamless' after hours
Best Drink Deals for Locals	Club Paradise Rick's Cabaret Crazy Horse III
Classiest Gourmet Dining	Treasures
Best Gourmet Food for Price	Badda Bing Rick's Cabaret
Best Bar Food Menus	Play It Again Sam Spearmint Rhino

Best of the Best Nude Clubs

Best Stage Dancers	Déjà Vu Little Darlings
Most Erotic Stage Show	Talk of the Town
Best Price on Lap Dances	Talk of the Town ($10)
Best Overall Deals for Locals	Little Darlings
Sexiest Weekly Show	Déjà Vu's oil wrestling (Sunday night)

Best of the Best Casino Shows	
Most Erotic Production Show	Crazy Horse Paris (MGM)
Runners-Up	Sin City Bad Girls (LV Hilton) Zumanity (NY-NY) Crazy Girls (Riviera)
Best of the Best Topless Pools	
Most Topless Women	Sapphire Pool (Rio)
Runners-Up	TAO Beach (Venetian) GO Pool (Flamingo)

Best of the Best

WEEKLY EVENTS		
DAY	**CLUB**	**EVENT OR SPECIAL DEAL**
Monday	Babes (nude)	Free admission w/military ID
	Little Darlings (nude)	Ladies and Couples $5 admission
Tuesday	Babes (nude)	2 laps for $30
	Badda Bing	Tuesday's Last Supper free buffet and $1 lap dances (6 p.m.-11 p.m.)
	Déjà Vu Showgirls (nude)	Twofer Tuesdays 2-for-1 lap dances
	Little Darlings (nude)	Amateur Strip Contest (12:30 a.m.)
Wednesday	Déjà Vu Showgirls (nude)	Amateur Contest
Thursday	Babes (nude)	Oil Wrestling (11:30 p.m. and 12:30 a.m.)
	Déjà Vu Showgirls (nude)	Locals night free admission, $5 drinks
	Palomino Club (nude)	Urban Nite (10:30 p.m.–3:30 a.m.)
Friday	Library (topless)	Shower shows
Saturday	Library (topless)	Shower shows
Sunday	Déjà Vu Showgirls (nude)	Oil Wrestling (1 a.m.)
	Little Darlings (nude)	Free admission w/military ID

5

Choosing A Strip Club Based On Your Budget

What if you have only $20 to spend on strip-club entertainment and you'd like a nice relaxing night of watching women take their clothes off? What if you have $50? $250? Which clubs are your best bets for value, visuals and action?

The answers depend on several factors, including whether or not you're a Nevada resident, how you arrive at the clubs, and if you pay a cover charge (for non-locals). Remember, if you're from out of town and you arrive in a cab, most clubs will hit you up for a hefty admission fee. So, let's get that issue out of the way first.

Cover Charges and Beer Prices

Clubs with no cover charge for locals or out-of-towners at any time: Chicas Bonitas, Club Platinum, Foxy Girls, Hustler Erotic Ultra Club, and Larry's Villa.

Clubs with relatively cheap cover charges for all: Library $5, Play It Again Sam $10, and Palomino Club no cover Sunday-Thursday.

Clubs with no cover charge for locals and/or those who don't arrive by cab: Badda Bing, Cheetahs, Club Paradise, Crazy Horse III, Play It Again Sam, Rick's Cabaret, Sapphire, Seamless, Spearmint Rhino, Treasures, and Velvet Lion.

Choosing A Strip Club Based On Your Budget

Of these, my personal recommendations for out-of-towners on a tight budget start with the Palomino Club. If it's not a Friday or Saturday night, this one's a no-brainer: Admission is free and a domestic beer is $6.50.

On weekend nights, I'd pay the $5 to get into the Library, where a beer will cost you $6. I like the Library much more than any of the free topless clubs (but this is on weekends only).

If you're a local, however, look at all the topless joints you can get into for free. If you stick with the major clubs where a beer costs less than $7, your choices, with one beer, include: Cheetahs $6.50, Hustler Erotic Ultra Club $2 (!), Play It Again Sam $5.25, Rick's Cabaret $5, and Velvet Lion $6.

My personal favorite among this group: Rick's Cabaret.

With More Money for Lap Dances

Now, say you've got a half-hour to kill and you'd like to go to a strip club, get a drink and a lap dance, then split. What will it cost you? Again, that depends on whether or not you're a Nevada resident (or, in some cases, you simply don't arrive in a cab). The chart on pg. 41 shows the cost of admission, drink, and lap dance for out-of-staters and locals. I've starred my personal favorites, but you should read the complete reviews of each club to see why they're my favorites; your criteria may differ from mine.

Also note: All costs in the charts on pages 41 and 43 are rounded to the nearest dollar, based on the best information I have, and assume that you're not drinking during happy hour, or on special reduced admission days, or when there are special discounts on lap dances, etc. Read the full reviews for tips on special prices that many clubs offer.

Note how much less locals pay than out-of-staters. Most of the cost difference is due to the free (or reduced) admission policy for locals at most clubs, though in some cases locals get reduced rates for drinks and even lap dances.

If you have budget concerns when it comes to your entertainment expenses, use the previous chart as a general guide to choosing a club.

COST OF ADMISSION + 1 DRINK + 1 LAP DANCE			
Out-of-State Residents		**Nevada Residents**	
Hustler Club**	$22	Crazy Horse III	$20
Larry's Villa	$24	★ Talk of the Town*	$22
Chicas Bonitas	$25	Hustler Club	$22
Foxy Girls	$25	Larry's Villa	$24
★ Talk of the Town*	$27	Chicas Bonitas	$25
★ Library	$31	Foxy Girls	$25
Play It Again Sam	$35	Play It Again Sam	$25
Babes*	$40	★ Rick's Cabaret	$25
Pussycat's*	$40	★ Cheetahs	$26
★ Little Darlings*	$45	Velvet Lion	$26
★ Seamless	$48	★ Treasures	$27
★ Déjà Vu*	$50	Club Paradise	$27
★ Palomino Club	$51	★ Seamless	$28
★ Sapphire	$52	★ Spearmint Rhino	$28
Sheri's Cabaret*	$55	★ Badda Bing	$29
Girls of Glitter Gulch	$55	Sheri's Cabaret*	$30
Velvet Lion	$56	Pussycat's*	$30
★ Cheetahs	$57	★ Little Darlings*	$30
Club Paradise	$57	Babes*	$30
Crazy Horse III	$57	★ Library	$31
★ Treasures	$57	★ Sapphire	$32
OG	$58	★ Palomino Club	$36
★ Rick's Cabaret	$58	OG	$38
★ Spearmint Rhino	$58	★ Déjà Vu*	$40
★ Badda Bing	$59	Girls of Glitter Gulch	$55

★ Personal favorites, applies to Friday and Saturday nights only

*non-alcoholic drinks only

**cost of the currently "negotiable" lap-dance price estimated at a standard $20

But always read the full reviews of the clubs you're considering. Paying a few extra bucks to go to a club that suits your personal tastes, as opposed to just picking the cheapest joint available, is often worth it.

If you've got more time and more money to spend, the chart on pg. 43 compares prices for two drinks and a half-hour in the VIP room. I assume that your two drinks are bought on the main floor of the club and if a bar tab is required for the VIP room, this is added on top of the drinks you consume before you go to the VIP. Again, my personal favorites are starred.

Lots of Lap Dances

The best deal on nude laps in Las Vegas is found at Talk of the Town, where all dances are $10 each. Little Darlings has nude laps for $20 and Sheri's Cabaret has nude laps *for locals* for $20. You'll have to pay $30-$35 for a nude lap dance at the other nude clubs that offer them. But some clubs have 2-for-1 specials on lap dances on various nights. See my full reviews for details.

As for lap dances at the topless joints, they're pretty much $20 across the board, though again, some clubs have 2-for-1 specials on certain nights. See the full reviews.

Lots of VIP Room Time

Far and away, your best bet for time in the VIP room is Play It Again Sam, where a half-hour is $100 and includes a bottle of champagne.

Your next best bet is Babes, where a half-hour is $150 and the dancer is nude.

At Talk of the Town, where the VIP room price is "negotiable," I got a half-hour nude for $199, with no bar-tab requirement (since there's no bar).

At all other clubs, nude or topless, expect to pay $200-$300 for a half-hour and at most clubs, a bar tab will be required in addition to this dancer fee.

Choosing A Strip Club Based On Your Budget

COST OF ADMISSION + 2 DRINKS + HALF-HOUR IN VIP			
Out-of-State Residents		**Nevada Residents**	
Play It Again Sam	$120	Play It Again Sam	$110
Babes*	$170	Babes*	$160
★ Library	$217	★ Talk of the Town*	$213
★ Talk of the Town*	$218	★ Library	$217
Sheri's Cabaret*	$245	★ Spearmint Rhino	$226
Velvet Lion	$262	Crazy Horse III	$227
Crazy Horse III	$264	Velvet Lion	$232
★ Spearmint Rhino	$266	Sheri's Cabaret*	$235
★ Palomino Club	$273	★ Palomino Club	$248
★ Seamless	$276	★ Seamless	$256
★ Cheetahs	$293	★ Cheetahs	$263
★ Sapphire	$294	★ Sapphire	$264
★ Badda Bing	$304	★ Badda Bing	$274
★ Treasures	$315	★ Treasures	$285
★ Déjà Vu*	$320	★ Rick's Cabaret	$310
Girls of Glitter Gulch	$320	Diamond Cabaret*	$310
Diamond Cabaret*	$320	★ Little Darlings*	$310
★ Little Darlings*	$325	★ Déjà Vu*	$310
★ Rick's Cabaret	$346	Girls of Glitter Gulch	$320
Club Paradise	$405	Club Paradise	$367
OG	$426	OG	$406

★ Personal favorites, applies to Friday and Saturday nights only
*non-alcoholic drinks only

Lots of VIP Room Time When Price Is No Object

Many VIP rooms in the topless clubs are crowded affairs where a dozen or more customers are crammed into a relatively small space with little privacy. If this appeals to you—for example, you like to

49

watch other dancers entertaining other customers while you're being entertained—your best bets are the most popular joints, like Cheetahs and Spearmint Rhino.

Clubs that offer more VIP-room privacy in less-cramped quarters are Badda Bing, Rick's Cabaret, Sapphire, and Treasures.

Other topless clubs where the selection of dancers is usually good on the weekends and where you may not be so crowded are the Library, OG, Seamless, and Velvet Lion.

Of the nude clubs, your best selection of dancers is at Déjà Vu and Little Darlings.

Palomino Club has a good selection and this is the only nude club where you can drink booze.

The most private nude VIP rooms are at Talk of the Town.

These clubs have no cover charge for locals or out-of-towners at any time: Chicas Bonitas, Club Platinum, Foxy Girls, Hustler Erotic Ultra Club, and Larry's Villa.

6

The Strip Club Ratings

At the bottom of the data boxes that lead off each of the club reviews in chapters 7 and 8, you'll see three ratings: "Grade of Club," "Grade of Dancer," and "SPW." Together, they provide a good quick glimpse into the quality of each club, but they're not 100% intuitive. Hence, each system is explained here. Yes, you can eyeball the ratings and get an idea of what you're in for at a given club, but understanding exactly what each grade represents will give you the deepest insight.

Grading the Clubs

Grading the clubs fairly, by using any single rating system, is not cut-and-dried. The topless clubs are primarily about lap dances and VIP rooms, so the quality of entertainment is highly dependent on the individual dancer. Five guys in the same club may have entirely different VIP-room experiences, even if they all pay the same price. And different guys are often looking for entirely different private shows.

For example, at one club, where an hour in the VIP costs $500, one dancer was trying to hard-sell me. The way she put it was, "Why pay some other girl five hundred for an air dance, when for five hundred with me, you can get laid?" I'm not into having sex in strip clubs, so even if I'd considered her the most gorgeous dancer I'd ever seen and

The Strip Club Ratings

I was sitting there with a few thousand bucks of mad money burning a hole in my pocket, I would have turned her down. Some other guy, however, might find an hour in the VIP with this dancer to be a great experience and a great value at $500. So there's no practical way for me to rate how good the VIP-room experience in any given club would be for you. (I should point out that a blatant solicitation for sex by a dancer in a strip club like this is a rare occurrence in Las Vegas.)

In my reviews, I primarily rate the strip clubs by their stage shows. I tell you the prices of the lap dances and VIP rooms and the bar tabs when applicable, and I describe how comfortable and/or how private these rooms are. But I don't attempt to rate how sexy the VIP-room dances are. Any time you go into a VIP room, there's an element of gamble in it. If I do comment on a VIP-room experience, it's because there was some special reason to—perhaps because the price was so low in comparison to other strip clubs or the accommodations or services were so unusual.

I also don't identify specific dancers in my reviews, as this would be a waste of ink. There are dozens of Tiffanys and Ashleys and Daisys and Bambis working in the Las Vegas strip clubs, and many of them move around from club to club regularly.

Now, with that said, there is one important grading criterion for the clubs. This has to do with the fact that the review descriptions apply to the clubs at peak times—weekends, prime hours, specialty nights, etc. As such, if you go to a place like the Library at 7 p.m. on a Tuesday, you probably won't find a bunch of hot babes romping in the shower that makes that club unique.

No matter what club you visit, you shouldn't expect to find a cream-of-the-crop roster filled with L.A., Burbank, San Diego, Phoenix, and Seattle "weekend warriors"—not to mention Las Vegas' finest—if you show up on a Wednesday. That's not to say that all the clubs are duds on weekdays. In fact, you can count on some of them to be strong most nights.

Basic strategy if you're out on a weekday is to stick to the clubs that are most popular with the locals. At the less popular clubs, your best bet is to visit on Friday or Saturday nights only. The charts that follow

52

The Strip Club Ratings

compile all the club grades and provide a general guide, but remember that even the best-rated clubs will be much more quiet earlier in the evening than they are from about 10 p.m. on.

GRADE A CLUB

MOSTLY ABOVE AVERAGE DANCERS EVERY NIGHT		
TOPLESS		**NUDE**
Cheetahs	Seamless	Babes
Club Paradise	Spearmint Rhino	Déjà Vu Showgirls
OG	Treasures	Little Darlings
Rick's Cabaret	Velvet Lion	Palomino Club
Sapphire		Sheri's Cabaret
		Talk of the Town

GRADE B CLUB

SOME ABOVE AVERAGE DANCERS BEST ON FRIDAY AND SATURDAY NIGHTS	
TOPLESS	
Badda Bing	Library
Crazy Horse III	Play It Again Sam

GRADE C CLUB

MAY OR MAY NOT HAVE ABOVE AVERAGE DANCERS ON ANY GIVEN NIGHT	
TOPLESS	
Chicas Bonitas	Girls of Glitter Gulch
Club Platinum	Hustler Erotic Ultra Club
Foxy Girls	Larry's Villa

GRADE D CLUB

NOT A REGULAR STRIP CLUB
NUDE
Can Can Room
Diamond Cabaret
Pussycat's

Grading the Dancers

My rating system for dancers in strip clubs is politically incorrect (as though anything else in this book could be considered politically correct!). It has absolutely nothing to do with dancing talent or any acrobatic ability the dancers might possess. It's based entirely on what they look like with their clothes off. The reason for this system is that most dancers in strip clubs—especially in the topless clubs—rarely have much opportunity to dance. Again, the stages are so small that dancing is simply not an option. (In my reviews, I mention which clubs have bigger and better stages, where you're more likely to see some dancing talent.)

I also realize that my opinion of physical attractiveness is entirely subjective. Your opinion may differ. I can go online right now and find hundreds of websites dedicated to sexy photos of naked women, ranging from the emaciated to the morbidly obese, from models who appear to be pubescent teenagers to wrinkled old grannies, and all of these sites must appeal to someone out there. Every type of female on the planet is some dude's fantasy. My tastes tend toward the traditional.

The reviews identify the clubs in which you'll likely find dancers who are older, or a bit more zaftig, or tipping the scales in the ass department. Do you prefer dancers who are black or Latina? Do you want to go where the locals go? I identify these clubs in the reviews, so you'll know where to find the types of dancers you're seeking.

But my dancer ratings for all clubs are based on how much the women look like professional dancers or athletes or models to me. And when I use "models" as a standard, I don't mean some scrawny anorexic from *Vogue* magazine. I'm thinking more of Victoria's Secret models—healthy-looking women whom most guys would like to see out of the lingerie they're modeling, or even in them. Similarly, when I use athletes as a standard, I don't mean the Russian women's weight-lifting squad. I'm thinking more of the type of girl who might be found competing in sports where physical grace and beauty are big factors—Olympic diving, collegiate gymnastics, professional figure skating. Even beach volleyball works for me. I wonder how many guys, flipping through the sports channels on TV, haven't stopped to watch a match or two when—zowie! Who are those babes in teeny bikinis leaping around on the sand with a beach ball?

Also, my rating system has nothing to do with breast size. This will disappoint a lot of guys who think it should be a major factor, but personally, I'm not a tit man and I find obvious boob jobs unattractive. A lot of dancers get breast-enhancement surgery, so I don't downgrade dancers with big tits or boob jobs because of my predilections. My reviews mention which clubs have high silicone factors and which don't, so you can make your own decisions on where to go, but my ratings are based more on the overall package.

Thanks to the Vegas market, with so many casino shows, strip clubs, and round-the-clock cocktail service, this city attracts huge numbers of attractive young women looking for work. And because working as a stripper pays so well—with many dancers making well into six digits annually—the competition for positions in the top clubs

is fierce. For us guys, this is great; we get to see incredibly gorgeous women dancing around with their clothes off. But it's also the reason why I'm pretty strict in my ratings. You don't have to watch less-than-gorgeous dancers in this town if you choose not to.

My rating system consists of five categories: Very fine, fine, average, below average, and desperate. These ratings are pretty descriptive in and of themselves, but for the sake of being perfectly clear, here's what they mean to me.

GRADING THE DANCERS	
VERY FINE	Absolutely gorgeous body. *Playboy/Penthouse* material. In all likelihood, she makes more money than you do.
FINE	Above average. No extraneous body fat. Any guy would want to do her.
AVERAGE	Girl-next-door type. Maybe not quite a Victoria's Secret model, but still pretty easy on the eyes when she's not wearing much. Let's face it, even an average girl in her twenties or early thirties looks awfully damn good with her clothes off.
BELOW AVERAGE	My below-average rating goes to dancers who are a bit too chunky, or maybe too skinny, with perhaps mild cellulite or breasts that are losing their youthful firmness. The typical below-average dancer would probably look better with more clothes on. You won't see these dancers very often in the top strip clubs. Guys who like heavy women might prefer some clubs where below-average dancers dominate the scene, so be sure to read the text of the reviews to see if the dancers are the right type for you. The single most common reason that I give any club's dancers a below-average rating is that the dancers are too heavy.
DESPERATE	My desperate rating is reserved for dancers who are way below average in physical appeal. In clubs that hire desperate dancers, you'll see obvious cellulite (and lots of it), inordinately drooping breasts and big belly folds or sagging skin all over. Desperate dancers are just not professional dancer/athlete/model material in my opinion. They seem to be women who have fallen on hard times and are doing what they can to make a buck.

Rating the Stage Shows: The SPW Scale

There are many criteria a reviewer might use to rate strip-club stage shows. Is there more than one stage? How big is the main stage? How good are the sound system and lighting? How good is the seating in regard to the stage?

I cover all these factors in my reviews, but I ultimately rate the stage shows—topless and nude—according to the single most important criterion for strip-club aficionados as recommended by the International Board of Strip Club Devotees: the "SPW Scale."

The SPW (or Statistical Probability of Wood) Scale ranges from a theoretical high of 100% (impossible to attain in the real world) down to an unlikely (but unfortunately attainable) rating of 0%. To be honest, a club's SPW rating is based on my subjective opinion of how sexy the stage shows are, which is to say, how likely I think it is that a show will turn you on. Obviously, the average grade of dancer in a club is a big factor in this. But a club with lots of fine and very fine dancers doesn't necessarily rate higher than one with mostly average girls. A small dark stage generally makes for a poor stage show. Therefore, most of the topless clubs, including many of the most popular clubs with the finest dancers, have pretty low SPW ratings for their stage shows.

An SPW rating of 80% or more means that, in my opinion, if you don't get turned

SPW: Statistical Probability of Wood

SPW rating range: 100% (impossible to attain in the real world) down to an unlikely (but unfortunately attainable) 0%.

on in this club most of the time you go there, then face it: You're gay. You're reading the wrong guidebook. Go to the Huntington Press website and you'll find the more appropriate guide, *Gay Vegas*. (And if you know you're not gay, then buy some Viagra, because IMHO, you have some serious circulation problems below the waist.) An SPW rating below 20% means that, in my opinion, this club is about as arousing as the Macy's Thanksgiving Day Parade. If you always get turned on in a club with a rating this low, you probably shouldn't be wasting your money in strip clubs. Just go home and watch TV. Technically, any SPW rating above 50% is pretty good. A club with a rating of exactly 50% is probably worth a look if you feel like flipping a coin with your erectile tissues.

Personally, I recommend not visiting a club with an SPW rating below 50%, unless you're going there specifically for the lap dances or VIP room, or because the club has some great deal on drinks or Monday Night Football or something like that.

Finally, strip clubs often change ownership and when they do, they often change their names. I mention the prior name(s) of any strip club that has changed in the past few years, so that visitors to Las Vegas who remember, but can't find, a club they visited will know if it now exists under a different name. However, this doesn't mean that the club is the same as the one you remember, as new owners often change policies, décor, schedules, prices, etc.

7

Reviewing the Topless Clubs

In the following pages, you'll find the reviews of all of Las Vegas' topless clubs, arranged alphabetically. Each includes a data box at the top with pertinent information about location and hours, a photograph of the club's exterior, and the three ratings discussed in Chapter 7: Grade of Club, Grade of Dancer, and SPW. None of the topless clubs are rated Grade D. As a quick refresher, Grades A, B, and C mean, respectively: good every night, good on the weekends, and, essentially, *good luck*.

Read the body of each review to get the inside scoop on prices, special events, and first-hand accounts and descriptions gathered during my multiple visits to the club.

You must be 21 to enter any topless club in Las Vegas, as all of these clubs serve alcoholic beverages.

BADDA BING!
(formerly Men's Club, formerly Leopard Lounge)
3500 W. Naples Dr., Las Vegas (#1 on map, pg. 39)

Phone: (702) 541-7000
Hours: noon–6 a.m.
Minimum Age: 21
Valet Parking: Yes; well-lit fenced lot with attendant and valet
Cover Charge: $30 after 6 p.m.; locals, free if arriving in own vehicle
Full Bar: Yes
Food: Yes; gourmet menu
Lap Dances: Main room, $20; VIP room, 3 songs/$100, half-hour/$200 + $50 bar tab, full hour/$400 + $100 bar tab; Private room, half-hour/$300 + $200 bar tab, full hour/$500 + $300 bar tab
Website: baddabinglv.com

Grade of Club: B
Grade of Dancer: Mostly average and fine, some below average
SPW: 25%

Snyder Says: Da ritziest VIP rooms in town!

This is not a joint where you should show up in your old Megadeth T-shirt, cut-off jeans, and flip-flops. That crystal chandelier hanging over the bar is the size of a Lamborghini and probably cost about the same. So hop into your Armani slacks, a fine silk shirt, and your Italian calf-skin loafers, and don't forget to put on your Patek Philippe watch.

If you remember the Leopard Lounge that closed in 2005, forget it. Everything about this club was renovated when the new owners took it over and turned it into the Men's Club. Recently, the owners changed the club's name again to that of the fictional New Jersey strip club run by mobsters on the HBO show, "The Sopranos." The fictional Bada Bing was a low-end dive; Badda Bing (note different spelling) in Las Vegas may be the most opulent club in Vegas. It's not the biggest in town by far, but it's definitely on the high end of plush.

Badda Bing has a wine cellar that boasts 10,000 bottles and an extensive gourmet-food menu. In addition to the standard offerings like sandwiches, burgers, salads, and wings, they offer steaks, salmon, shrimp, pastas, and many other items beyond bar fare. All entrees are reasonably priced. The dinner items are the best I've ever had in a strip joint. Seared salmon, stir-fried veggies, and steamed rice is priced at

Badda Bing may be the most opulent strip club in Las Vegas, but beers are less than $10 downstairs.

$16, and everything is perfectly prepared. High-end food at a low-end price, and in truly elegant surroundings—you can't beat that.

The club has its own kitchen on premises, but no dedicated dining area. Meals are served at small cocktail tables in the main room, where you can watch the stage dancers while the guy sitting next to you may be getting a lap dance. Anyone dining with a friend or a small group will have to pull together multiple tables.

But let's get to the important stuff ...

Bad Timing, or Victim of the "Taxi Wars?"

For more than a year, Badda Bing was operating primarily as a VIP-room club, with one small stage that had few rail seats. The stage wasn't easily visible from much of the room, as the central bar blocked the view. This was a classy lap-dance club you went to when you were in the mood for a really great bottle of wine to enjoy with a beautiful woman—with its great selection of both—in the most elegant strip-club surroundings in town, definitely an experience you should try at least once when you've got a thousand bucks to blow.

But the club recently underwent an expansion in which two more stages, both bigger and lower, were added, with lots of rail seats. A new downstairs VIP area was added with another full bar. I must admit, the club looks better than ever. It might be the swankiest club in Vegas.

Now, it remains to be seen if this club can make a comeback.

Check out the cool couches in Badda Bing's VIP rooms.

Prior to the renovation, Badda Bing had lots of gorgeous dancers. During the renovation, which took months longer than expected, the club stopped paying cabbies for drop-offs and they lost not only the tourist trade, but most of their local customers as well. The dancer quality went down, but the club couldn't financially justify paying cabbies to bring them customers when they were operating at half-speed. I had to downgrade this club from Grade A to Grade B, based on the loss of their hottest dancers, but I'm hopeful that they'll rise again to their prior standards now that the club is looking so grand. Badda Bing has big plans to host special events and even bring in feature performers in order to get their dancers and customers back.

The VIP rooms on the second level of the club are dimly lit by wall sconces, with big comfortable couches and

Two new stages should enhance Badda Bing's rail appeal.

lots of tapestry pillows, far above the norm. There's also another full bar upstairs, but all drinks on the second level are priced at $13 each, so don't go to upstairs just to have a beer that would cost you only $9 downstairs.

The Excuse Booth

One feature this club offers that I haven't seen elsewhere is an "excuse booth." Let's say you're supposed to be at work in ten minutes, but you've just met a dancer you'd like to take into the VIP room for a half-hour. No problem. You go into the excuse booth—which is about the size of a phone booth, with a video monitor where the phone would be, and you close the door behind you. You pull up the "traffic-jam" sound effects, turn up the volume, and call your boss on your cell phone. Amidst the honking horns of the angry drivers, you calmly explain to your boss that a big rig has overturned on I-15 and it looks like you'll be an hour late.

Ten different sound-effect backgrounds are available. In addition to the traffic jam, you can place yourself in a hospital emergency room, casino, restaurant, airport terminal, convention, subway, bowling alley, supermarket, even at a boxing match or poolside. Each sound screen comes with a list of pre-fab excuses that scroll on the video screen, in case you can't think up a good excuse on your own as to why you happen to be in a hospital or at the airport, etc.

Listen to daytime radio in Las Vegas and you'll hear this joint's now-famous slogan: "I'll take care of that thing at the Bing!"

The Shower Show Upstairs

Many Badda Bing customers are unaware that the club also has a shower stage upstairs across from the far end of the bar. That's because the club rarely uses it—though they did use it for their Super Bowl party in 2009. I've never seen it in operation, so I can't review the show itself for you. According to the marketing director, they do plan to use it more frequently in the future, possibly every weekend. Watch SinCityAdvisor.com for details.

CHEETAHS
2112 Western Ave., Las Vegas (#2 on map, pg. 39)

Phone: (702) 384-0074
Hours: 24/7
Minimum Age: 21
Valet Parking: Yes; well-lit lot with doorman out front
Cover Charge: $20 if arriving in own vehicle; $30 if arrving by cab or limo; locals, free
Full Bar: Yes
Food: Yes; free pizza and/or wings in the afternoon
Lap Dances: Main room, $20; VIP room, 3 songs/$100; G-Spot Room, half-hour/$250, no bar tab required, full hour/$500, no bar tab required
Website: cheetahsnv.com

Grade of Club: A
Grade of Dancer: Mostly fine, some very fine, some average
SPW: 45%

Snyder Says: Do these babes look good?
Who knows? They sure feel good!

When I want a lap dance, I go to Cheetahs. It's a no-brainer.

Lap dance?

Cheetahs.

Simple as that.

When you first walk into this club, you stand there for a minute or two waiting for your eyes to adjust to the darkness. Then it hits you—they won't be adjusting. It's pitch fucking black in here!

All the modern gentlemen's clubs are dark. We guys like dark, especially when we've got an itch for a lap dance. Unfortunately, most joints get it wrong. Their idea of dark is a bunch of flashing blue and red lights. It's dark, more or less, but it's irritating. Who wants flashing lights? Has anyone (other than Michael Jackson) ever had flashing lights installed in his own home?

No.

Case closed.

The Art of Darkness

Cheetahs, on the other hand, does darkness right. They've got dark down to an art form. Subdued violet tube lighting runs along the ceiling. That's it. The feeling of the place is something like a high-school make-out party. This is lap-dance heaven.

Let's say I'm getting a lap dance and the pastor of my church is getting a lap dance in the seat right next to me. Hey, I wouldn't know it and neither would he. It's too fucking dark.

What if the girl in my lap is ugly? No problem. Can't see her.

The stage lighting isn't a whole lot brighter than the overall club lighting. They do have flashing red and blue lights over the stage, but they're not bright and there aren't very many of them.

So it's kind of hard to judge the beauty and talent of the dancers, but I think this is a topless club. I remember one time when the little blue stage light flashed and I saw a couple of knockers. Big ones. Either that, or a couple of bald guys were standing in front of the stage.

Anyway, this place is crowded in the evenings. Packed. But you won't have any problem getting a lap dance. Cheetahs gets not only the Darkest Club in Vegas Award, but the Jan-and-Dean Award too—two girls for every boy! Just be careful, when you're looking for a seat, that you don't happen to sit in some guy's lap. This can happen if he's some goth freak wearing black clothes. On the other hand, he might slip you $20 before he realizes you're not a girl.

Excellent club.

Dracula says: "Five stars."

Cheetahs' website says they have a free lunch from noon to 4 p.m. What this means is that sometime between noon and 4 p.m.—and maybe more like 1 or 2 p.m.—they come up with some free pizza and/or chicken wings. Not bad, but don't think you can just go there at noon and get a free lunch. There's not really a lunch buffet or menu.

The club has a big main stage and two smaller stages. They're all dimly lit, but you can sit on the rail and watch the dancers comfortably; the few flashing lights aren't irritating. As pointed out above, however, this is primarily a lap-dance club, not much of a club for watching dancers on stage.

CHICAS BONITAS
(formerly Cheerleaders, formerly Satin Saddle)
1818 Las Vegas Blvd. N. (#3 on map, pg. 39)

Phone: (702) 256-7894
Hours: Sun.–Wed. 11 a.m.–2 a.m.,Thurs.–Sat. 11 a.m.–4 a.m.
Minimum Age: 21
Valet Parking: No; seedy neighborhood, but located across from a casino on well-trafficked street
Cover Charge: Thurs.–Sat. $5 after 7 p.m.; locals, free
Full Bar: Yes
Food: No
Lap Dances: Main room, $20; VIP room, $35, no bar tab required
Website: None

Grade of Club: C
Grade of Dancer: Fine, average, and below average
SPW: 30%

Snyder Says: Casa de tetas y culo.

The sound system's new, but I can't understand a word the DJ's saying. *No entiendo español.* A stunningly gorgeous black dancer steps up onto the low-platform runway stage to the right of the bar, but no seats are available on the rail, so I sit on a barstool to watch her. The hip-hop music starts cranking, but I have no idea what the song is or who is singing it. This is Mexican hip-hop, in Spanish. Then I notice the TV monitor overhead. There's a soccer game on. On the other side of the central bar is another stage, this one a low circular platform where a hot buxom señorita with jet black hair and deep olive skin is down on her knees, teasing the guys on the rail by squeezing her titties together, but not quite freeing them from the red-lace tube top she's wearing.

"Do you want a dance?"

I look up to see the girl who's just spoken the first words in English I've heard since entering this place. She's a pretty blond in a white-lace cat suit, with big tits and ample hips.

Welcome to Chicas Bonitas, Las Vegas' first Latino strip club.

If you remember the old Satin Saddle, which for a short time became Cheerleaders, forget it. Chicas Bonitas (which means "Beautiful Girls") has been completely renovated. It's not a dark high-tech gentlemen's club in the modern mode, but more of a fairly well-lit sports bar with topless entertainment. It's a small club with a central bar and two stages. The bar opens at 5 p.m., but the dancers don't start until 8 p.m.

There's a dancer on each stage, so you can move from one side of the bar to the other if you have a preference for one of the dancers. They're an even mix of white, black, and Latina, and you definitely see more hefty girls here than in the major Vegas topless clubs, so if you like women with a bit more padding on their hips and thighs, you'll like this club.

Lap dancing out on the main floor costs the usual $20 per song. In the VIP area, a private curtained area with booths at the back of the club, a lap dance is $35.

This is really just a friendly neighborhood titty bar for the North Las Vegas guys. If you like black and Latina girls and a wider range of body types than you see in the major Vegas clubs, you'll like this place, even if you can't understand the DJ when he's announcing 2-for-1 specials.

CLUB PARADISE
4416 Paradise Rd., Las Vegas (#4 on map, pg. 39)

Phone: (702) 734-7990
Hours: Mon.–Fri. 5 p.m.–8 a.m., Sat.–Sun. 6 p.m.–8 a.m.
Minimum Age: 21
Valet Parking: Yes; valet parking only, no self-parking
Cover Charge: $30; locals, free
Full Bar: Yes
Food: No
Lap Dances: Main room, $20; VIP room, half-hour/$260 + $100 bar tab, full hour/$500 +$100 bar tab; Crystal Room, half-hour/$260 + $200 bar tab, full hour/$500 +$200 bar tab
Website: clubparadise.net

Grade of Club: A
Grade of Dancer: Mostly fine, some very fine, some average
SPW: 30%

Snyder Says: Tourists in lap-dance limbo.

About two weeks prior to the 2008 presidential election, Club Paradise garnered some national attention by hosting a Sarah Palin look-alike contest. A couple dozen strippers competed in both bikini and debating competitions (seriously!), with the winner getting $10,000 and an all-expenses-paid trip to the inauguration in 2009. You can find some amusing videos of the contest on Youtube. So Club Paradise immediately gets high marks in my book for creativity and humor. But what's the club like on "normal" nights?

Club Paradise runs lots of promotions and parties—it's one of Las Vegas' go-to clubs for Monday Night Football.

When you first walk into this place, it looks like just another generic, dark, high-end, high-tech gentlemen's club. Strippers 'R' Us. There's a dancer with the requisite boob job wiggling around on a tiny elevated stage close to the entrance and you can see another dancer on the main stage in the distance who's got a bit more room to move. You weave your way through the closely packed black-granite tables and leopard-print-upholstered chairs filled with guys, some of them getting lap dances, and you're pleased to see that despite the crowd, seats are available on the main-stage rail. You probably noticed as you worked your way through the crowd that the silicone factor in this club is high. Guys who like big tits will appreciate the selection.

The dancer on stage immediately walks up to you and, as you're digging through your wallet for some dollar bills to tip her, you realize that in order to see her, you have to lean back in your chair and crane your neck; unlike the chest-high stages you find in most strip clubs, this one is about a foot higher, right at eye level. If you don't tip your head back to look at the dancer, who's now towering over you, you're looking at her feet. When she gets down to do her floor work, however, you have to admit it's not a bad view at all. The only real problem now is the lighting …

Dancers dislike white spotlights (which provide the best stage lighting), because they're so hot to work under. Most topless clubs use red and blue spots, usually quite a few of them, flashing haphazardly. But Club Paradise has opted to forego most of the reds and just stick to blues. Blue's a problem, not only because it's dimmer than red—so that the stage dancer fades into the darkness—but also because blue lighting tends to make the dancers look like ghouls.

You decide to put up with the blue-skinned dancer—hey, you always had the hots for Lily Munster!—and you toss another dollar onto the stage, because her floor work is so sexy. She's doing everything she can to give you a good show for your money—literally coming over the rail to tease you as close up as possible—when suddenly bright white overhead spots start swirling, temporarily blinding you. You can't even look in the direction of the stage. What's happening? Police raid?

Okay, so the lighting technician is a sadist. Otherwise, this club has a great drink special for locals. If you have a Nevada driver's license and you show it to the bartender, you get two drinks for the price of one. Two domestic beers for $7.50 is about as cheap as you'll ever see in a strip club, and this deal is on 24/7 and applies to as many drinks as you want. The policy isn't posted at the bar to my knowledge, but it's been in force for many years.

Because of its location—right across the street from the Hard Rock Casino—Club Paradise attracts not only a lot of locals who come for the 2-for-1 beers, but a lot of tourists as well, including a fair number of couples who look like they're from flyover land and appear to feel totally out of place in a lap-dance club. The presence of this tourist element tends to keep the lap dancing in the main room pretty tame on the weekends, compared to clubs like Cheetahs or Rhino, where gaping tourists don't show up much.

You'll find a much nicer mini-stage and atmosphere in the Crystal Room—Club Paradise's VIP room—where the lighting is subdued and the stage height is perfect. Uncomfortable tourists are far less likely to be in there, thanks to the $200-minimum bar tab. Unfortunately, there's often no dancer on the Crystal Room stage. And in addition to the bar tab, lap dances in the Crystal Room will run you $260 per half-hour or $500 per hour. Right outside the Crystal Room is another less-private VIP area where lap dances cost the same, but the bar tab is only $100.

Club Paradise has valet parking only. A lot of the club's local customers self-park in the Hard Rock's parking lot and walk across the street. This might be convenient if you're actually gambling or partying at Hard Rock, but if you're coming from somewhere else in town, just give your car to the Club Paradise valet at the front door. It's fast and convenient and when you leave, you'll have your car delivered to you in about a minute. A $2 tip is sufficient for valet service anywhere in Vegas.

To sum up: convenient location. Great drink deal for locals. The main stage show is not all that great and lap dances out in the main room are sometimes constrained by the presence of appalled tourists. But there's a nice VIP room if you can afford it and some pretty good-looking dancers.

Reviewing the Topless Clubs

CLUB PLATINUM
(formerly Tender Trap)
311 E. Flamingo Rd., Las Vegas (#5 on map, pg. 39)

Phone: (702) 732-1111
Hours: Sun.–Thurs. 6 p.m.–4 a.m., Fri. and Sat. 6 p.m.–6 a.m.
Minimum Age: 21
Valet Parking: No; located on well-trafficked street
Cover Charge: None
Full Bar: Yes
Food: No
Lap Dances: Main room, $20; VIP booths, 3 songs/$120
Website: clubplatinum.com

Grade of Club: C
Grade of Dancer: Mostly average and below average, some fine
SPW: 25%

Snyder Says: If strip joints were puppies,
Club Platinum would be the runt of the litter.

74

Not too many years ago when this place was called the Tender Trap, it was just a little locals titty bar with one small stage, two or three dancers, and a jukebox. Now, the jukebox has been replaced by a DJ, the lighting has been redone to the modern gentlemen's-club standard—very dark, with the requisite flashing red and blue spots—and the main floor area is crammed with comfy lap-dance chairs. Lap dances cost the usual $20 per song and there's a more private VIP section of booths against one wall where you can get three lap dances for $120. Eight to ten dancers now work here on the weekends, instead of two or three. The net result? It's still just a little locals titty bar.

This whole club is about the size of my kitchen and gets maybe 20 customers on a weekend night. It's pretty well located, so I'm sure it gets a few tourists who see the joint when they're just driving by on Flamingo. As for the remodel job, I'm not crazy about the throbbing, flashing, high-tech gentlemen's-club look to begin with, but there's something deeply wrong with this motif in a place about the size of a der Wienerschnitzel. This club gets the "Smallest High-Tech Gentlemen's Club in Vegas" award. It's like a miniature of a real gentlemen's club. When Doctor Evil is cavorting with the lap dancers at Sapphire, you can be sure Mini-Me is right at home at Club Platinum.

CRAZY HORSE III
(formerly Penthouse Club, formerly Sin)
3525 W. Russell Rd., Las Vegas (#12 on map, pg. 39)

Phone: (702) 673-1700
Hours: 24/7
Minimum Age: 21
Valet Parking: Yes; well-lit lot with attendants outside
Cover Charge: None
Full Bar: Yes
Food: See description
Lap Dances: Main room, $20; VIP room, 3 songs/$100 + 2 drinks, half-hour/$200 + 2 drinks, full hour/$400 + 2 drinks; Private room, full hour/$500 + $300 bottle
Website: vegasalliance.com/crazyhorse3

Grade of Club: B
Grade of Dancer: Mostly fine and average, some very fine, some below average
SPW: 45%

Snyder Says: Has Crazy Horse arisen
from the ashes ... again?!

Drink for free! You betcha! Six hours a day, five days a week, no strings attached!

Crazy Horse III is on the warpath to get customers.

From 3 to 9 p.m. Monday through Friday, all domestic beers and well drinks are *free*. It's a good thing this review is appearing in *Topless Vegas*, as opposed to *Drunken Vegas*, or every lush in town would be there. Also, sporadically through the same hours, free food is brought in for the customers. One day it might be pizza, the next day, pasta and salad ... This is the best comp available in Vegas today. It beats any freebies offered in the casinos and there's no gambling requirement.

Up until June 2009, this was the Penthouse Club and under that name it struggled to lure the locals from the more popular clubs that have been in business for many years. The club initially opened in 2005 under the name Sin, but it never got off the ground. In sheer size, it's one of the biggest clubs in Vegas, but it was so poorly designed that it never attracted much of a crowd. The main stage was surrounded by the main bar, and to make matters worse, a two-foot-high Plexiglas barrier surrounded the stage, so when the dancer did her floor work, you were watching her through a window.

The Remodel Transformed the Club

But Penthouse changed all that. They put a big stage right in the center of the main room and, thanks to the low height and number of rail seats, it was definitely one of the better stages for watching dancers. For a while, it looked like Penthouse would become a real player in the Vegas strip-club scene, having lured a lot of the top dancers from the major clubs. They also started a generous VIP club for locals that allowed us to get our first drink free on every visit. Unfortunately, this was another club that couldn't afford the "taxi wars that really heated up in 2008. Unable to pay the drop-off fees the popular clubs were paying to cabbies, Penthouse lost much of its tourist trade, then its best dancers, and many of its local customers. On the less-crowded week nights especially, dancer quality was well below *Penthouse* magazine standards. Despite the club's name, *Penthouse* magazine money was not behind the venture. The owners were simply paying Penthouse a franchise fee to use the name. That fee wasn't insignificant and with the taxi wars on, it became clear that the brand was just another expense the club couldn't afford.

So in June 2009, the club was reincarnated as Crazy Horse III, with generous and aggressive new policies. It still remains to be seen if Crazy Horse III can compete with the big boys, but they're definitely going after the locals with this free-food-and-drink offer. It's too early to pass judgment as this is written two weeks later, but with free booze six hours a day, they should start to see some crowds, and this may bring back a lot of the top dancers. Watch SinCityAdvisor.com for updates. If the dancer quality goes up, we'll raise their club rating from Grade B to Grade A.

In Vegas, the name Crazy Horse has a long colorful history and the owners may be hoping it has some kind of magic that will bring in the customers. The Crazy Horse Saloon on Paradise Road was one of the most popular topless bars for decades. It closed in the late 1980s—but

not before its sister club, Crazy Horse Too, opened on Industrial Road. (See pages 31-35 for a discussion of the 2004 arrest and prosecution of 13 Crazy Horse Too dancers that inevitably led to the Nevada Supreme Court's decision legalizing "fondling and caressing" during lap dances.) Crazy Horse Too, which closed in 2006 at the height of its popularity when it lost its liquor license, had been lap-dance central in Vegas and was packed every night. Known for having some of the most gorgeous dancers anywhere and the highest-mileage VIP rooms in town, for more than two decades this was *the* strip club in Vegas for seeing and being seen. During the investigation into the club's tax-evasion charges, among the customers of the club interviewed by the feds were Robert De Niro, George Clooney, and Joe Pesci. When this club died, thousands of locals and visitors were stunned.

So is Crazy Horse III the reincarnation of Crazy Horse Too? Although one of the managers at Crazy Horse III was formerly a floor manager at Crazy Horse Too, there really isn't any other connection to the prior club. Will the locals and visitors who mourned the loss of their favorite topless joint will be hypnotically drawn to Crazy Horse III? With free booze five days a week, it could happen.

The design of the club itself is excellent: big stage, decent lighting, good sound system, and comfy lap-dance seats in darker areas of the main room away from the central stage. After 9 p.m., a domestic beer costs $9—on the high side, but still competitive with a lot of the plush joints.

The VIP room prices are also pretty standard, with a two-drink minimum (at $15 each). One of the rooms is very dark, even for a VIP room, and both of the rooms now have partitions between the booths for more privacy. A private room with a dancer for one hour is $500, with a $300 bottle fee. But this is a truly private room with a curtain that closes at the doorway. These rooms compete with the best VIP rooms available in Vegas for both comfort and privacy.

Technically, Crazy Horse III is part of a three-club conglomerate known as the Playground that's just now getting off the ground. It includes not only the gentlemen's club, but a combination sushi bar/rock club and an afterhours club with a live DJ.

The Dead Man's Hand sushi bar is located inside the Rock Room, which opens at 11 p.m. Tuesday through Sunday. Live local bands provide the music, with no cover charge. The Obsession afterhours club opens at 2 a.m. Tuesday, Thursday, Friday and Saturday, also with no cover charge, and it stays open officially until 7 a.m., but often keeps rocking until later, depending on when the late night clubbers start to filter out.

Obsession has been in operation for almost a year now and already has a following. If you're into the afterhours club scene, don't expect to hear mainstream music, classic rock, or top 40 at Obsession. This is all underground tech-house, techno, electro, trance, and breakbeats. In order to get into the Rock Room or Obsession, you have to go through the strip club. Very weird. But with no cover charges, late-night sushi, top DJs, and live bands, both of these clubs are already attracting crowds.

The Amateur Bikini Contest

The weekly bikini contest has been temporarily put on hold, but sources inside the club tell me it will return. Formerly held on Sunday nights at midnight, dancers complained that it was detracting from business on that night (which is typically a good night for dancers to earn tips). Watch the SinCityAdvisor website for details on when it returns. The bikini contest was open to all women who wanted to compete for $5,000 in cash and prizes. Locals got all drinks for half-price during the contest, and women who competed got all drinks free all night long. It's unclear whether these policies will continue.

The night I attended, there were 11 women in the contest and every one of them was really hot—great bodies (lots of boob jobs), young, pretty. They all had such classic bikini bodies I had the feeling the show's producers had brought them in (and I don't mean that as a complaint). All were wearing skimpy thong bikinis. The MC's mike didn't work all that great, so I couldn't understand a lot of what he was saying, especially since the DJ never turned down the hip-hop music.

From what I was able to make out, the contest was sponsored by a swimsuit company, so I suspect all the girls were wearing the sponsor's suits. (Personally, I'm waiting for Wicked Weasel to start sponsoring swimsuit competitions.) The

MC brought the contestants out one (or sometimes two) at a time, and they each got a minute or so to strut and pose. Some seemed to know a few stripper moves, but most were not professional dancers. A few had gimmicks. One girl came out with boxing gloves on. None of the contestants took their tops off, but two girls came out together with just their bikini bottoms on, wearing dollops of whipped cream on their nipples.

All contestants were introduced by first name only and were described as teachers or nurses or personal trainers or therapeutic masseuses, not dancers or strippers. There's something unusual about having a bikini contest in a topless joint, since the regular stage dancers wear less than the contestants. But I must admit the bikini girls were gorgeous, so I don't think the audience minded the PG-13-rated contest. I sure didn't.

But here's something I don't get. Why do so many strip clubs name themselves after a Native American hero most famous for defeating Custer at Little Big Horn? What did he ever do to be associated with topless dancers? In all existing photos of Crazy Horse, he has his shirt on. But the first Crazy Horse strip joint opened in Paris in 1951 (still in operation!), and today Crazy Horse gentlemen's clubs can be found in San Francisco, Chicago, Cleveland, Philadelphia, Miami, Anchorage, Atlanta, probably a dozen other cities in America, and even Panama! In any case, there's a new Crazy Horse in Vegas, our third one (or fourth, if you count the *Crazy Horse Paris* show at the MGM Grand), and up until 9 p.m., the drinks are on the Horse!

FOXY GIRLS

3013 S. Highland Dr., Las Vegas (#6 on map, pg. 39)

Phone: (702) 735-5750
Hours: 3 p.m.–3 a.m.; dancers start at 8 p.m., Fri. at 5 p.m.
Minimum Age: 21
Valet Parking: No; lot is private and well-lit
Cover Charge: Two drink minimum
Full Bar: Yes
Food: No
Lap Dances: $20
Website: None

Grade of Club: C
Grade of Dancer: Mostly average and below average
SPW: 20%

Snyder Says: Tits, ass, washers and dryers …

This is another only-in-Vegas joint, strictly a locals club with a small stage, pool table, and TV monitors for watching sports events. I stopped in one Saturday night a few years ago as I was driving by. The first thing I noticed was the big sign on the door: "MUST SHOW USA ID." The same notice was posted inside the door. Interesting. We now have a strip club that won't admit Canadians.

The next thing that hit me was the guy checking IDs at the entrance, a kindly looking old coot in a casual shirt—not a muscle-bound gorilla in a bad-fitting tuxedo who typically works the door at strip joints. Not only that—I recognized this guy, but I just couldn't place him.

At the bar, I picked up a business card for the club and the mystery was solved. The card said: "John Herda's Foxy Girls." I ran outside to verify it. Damn! This strip joint was built in the parking lot of Herda's Discount Appliance Warehouse (another locals joint). I'd bought a dishwasher from this guy a couple years ago!

For some reason, this endeared me to Foxy Girls. I just liked John Herda's gumption. Discount appliances by day, discount strip joint by night. The man never slept! Sadly, in August 2006, John Herda was killed in his home during a burglary. He was 83 years old.

Anyway, if you're not a local, don't waste your time. Small club, small stage, five-buck beers, and so-so dancers. But no cover, a one-drink minimum, and for some unknown reason—no Canadians.

GIRLS OF GLITTER GULCH
22 Fremont St., Las Vegas (#7 on map, pg. 39)

Phone: (702) 385-4774
Hours: Mon.–Fri. 1 p.m.–4 a.m., Sat. and Sun. 1 p.m.–5 a.m.
Minimum Age: 21
Valet Parking: No; just use any of the downtown casino lots
Cover Charge: Before 8 p.m. two drink minimum; after 8 p.m. $20, two drinks included
Full Bar: Yes
Food: No
Lap Dances: Main room, $35; VIP room, 3 songs/$100, half-hour/$300, full hour/$500
Website: None

Grade of Club: C
Grade of Dancer: Mostly average and below average, a few fine, some desperate
SPW: 15%

Snyder Says: Ghosts of G-Strings Past …

Reviewing the Topless Clubs

Welcome to Fabulous Las Vegas' Topless Dancer Graveyard. This downtown joint may be the most popular Vegas strip club where you're least likely to find a local. The Girls of Glitter Gulch survives almost 100% on the tourist trade and it does a lot of business in its prime Fremont Street location.

This club has a $20 cover charge for all—including any locals dumb enough to show up here—which includes your admission fee and your first two drinks. As soon as you get two feet inside the door, you're met by a waitress who seats you, takes your drink order, and quickly brings both drinks at once.

About the time you get your drinks, your eyes have grown accustomed to the darkness, and you're wondering why neither of the two dancers on the runway stage, nor any that are circulating through the crowd, look like the hot babes on the video marquee outside.

Before your eyes can adjust any further, a lady in lingerie appears at your side and says, "Do you want a dance?"

If you ask her how much a lap dance is, she'll tell you $35, but you probably won't ask. This is a club where dancers go when their chests start to sag and their guts get paunchy and the cellulite on their thighs starts to pucker. There are some good-looking dancers here, but too many of the dancers here wouldn't make the cut in any other club.

This may sound downright sexist and mean of me, but how would women feel if they thought they were going to see the *Chippendales* and instead got a bunch of fat balding guys in thongs doing the beer-barrel polka? Wouldn't they want their money back? Fuck political correctness. In my opinion, dancers are supposed to be attractive and talented. That's the job, man. That's the job.

Welcome to Fabulous Las Vegas' Topless Dancer Graveyard!

In Las Vegas, you can't believe everything you read!

HUSTLER EROTIC ULTRA CLUB
(formerly CHEZ MOI)
3131 Ponderosa Way, Las Vegas (#8 on map, pg. 39)

Phone: (702) 795-3131
Hours: 8 p.m.–4 a.m.
Minimum Age: 21
Valet Parking: No; private lot is well-lit
Cover Charge: None
Full Bar: Yes
Food: No
Lap Dances: Main room, $20; VIP room, 3 songs/$100
Website: None

Grade of Club: C
Grade of Dancer: Average
SPW: 25%

Snyder says: The blueprints are more interesting
than the stage show.

Yes, this is another Hustler Club, managed by the Déjà Vu chain. Larry Flynt, the notorious porn king and hero to all freedom-of-speech advocates (he was once quoted as saying, "I took a bullet for the First Amendment"), has a dozen or so Hustler Clubs around the U.S., as well as in the U.K. and Australia. I've been to his clubs in San Diego, San Francisco, and New Orleans. They're class joints. The current Las Vegas venue, on Ponderosa Way, is just temporary housing until the real club is built. A few years ago, a strip club in this same location, Chez Moi, never quite got off the ground and closed shortly after it opened. Flynt purchased the club and the huge tract of land adjacent to it on Dean Martin Drive, where he has recently broken ground for the multi-level club he's now building.

Like his other clubs, this will be a swank high-end affair. The blueprints for the new digs are posted on the wall in the temporary Ponderosa venue and it appears the Las Vegas Hustler Club will have a pool on the roof! So the Sapphire Pool at the Rio may end up with some real competition—but not until the summer of 2010 at the earliest, as I would expect it to be at least a year until the construction on this mammoth place is completed. Until then, we've got the temporary Hustler Club in the old Chez Moi building, so let's take a look at that.

The most notable feature of this club is the $2 price of all domestic beers and well drinks, every day during all hours of operation. That's about as cheap as drinking at home. There's also no admission charge for anyone. The club finally got a marquee out front that can be seen from the highway, so they've started to pick up a few more customers. At present, this is just a dive bar with cheap drinks and a few so-so topless dancers. There's a three-pole stage and decent lighting, but on slow nights you may sit through long stretches without a dancer on stage simply because both dancers and customers are sparse.

It's possible that with the Hustler brand name, even this little temporary facility will start drawing crowds, but that has yet to be seen. Since Déjà Vu is managing the club, you'll sometimes see some of the Déjà Vu or Little Darlings dancers on the Hustler stage and that's not a bad thing. Currently, the club isn't charging dancers a stage fee and customers can negotiate with dancers for the cost of a lap dance or private show. A small, one-couch, VIP room is in one corner of the club.

LARRY'S VILLA
2401 W. Bonanza Rd., Las Vegas (#9 on map, pg. 39)

Phone: (702) 647-2713
Hours: 24/7
Minimum Age: 21
Valet Parking: No; dicey neighborhood, located in strip mall behind 24-hour Chevron station and Popeye's Chicken on busy intersection
Cover Charge: None
Full Bar: Yes
Food: No
Lap Dances: VIP room, $20
Website: None

Grade of Club: C
Grade of Dancer: Mostly average, some below average
SPW: 35%

Snyder Says: Just a neighborhood titty bar with no pretensions.

Reviewing the Topless Clubs

This is a Cheers-type bar in a blue-collar neighborhood. The club is very casual, with a T-shirt and jeans crowd, and the stage dancers all look like neighborhood girls. No silicone in here. The dancers, mostly cute girls in their twenties, have a sweet attitude and they all get tipped on stage. The neighborhood boys like the neighborhood girls, especially when they show their titties. None of them are great dancers and you wouldn't see any in the top-end clubs. They're an equal mix of white, black, and latina, and there's a fair amount of excess body fat on a few of them. A number of older women also work the crowd for lap dances. I haven't seen these older women dance on stage. Lap dances occur in the VIP room only, not out on the main floor. The two women who tend bar in the evenings are generally the hottest-looking babes in the club; they don't get on stage, but they're tipped well too.

The decor here isn't pretentious. There's an old-fashioned runway stage and the lighting is much better than in most topless joints. No flashy high-tech "gentlemen's club" crap here—I doubt any of the customers in here would ever refer to themselves as "gentlemen." These are bikers and truck drivers and tradesmen just sitting around having some beers with their buds after work.

Larry's Villa is the oldest topless club in Las Vegas, operating in the same location since 1972. The founder, Larry LaPenta, died a couple years ago at the age of 84. He was a real character and in the last couple years before his death, he started a storefront non-denominational church—Thomas Paine's Church of God and Common Sense. He may have been the only person in America who simultaneously owned and operated both a church and a strip club. Only in Las Vegas …

I like this place, which doesn't pretend to be anything it's not. It's a titty bar with cute topless dancers, cheap beer, and no cover charge. If you're not crazy about the dancer on stage, you can play video poker on the bartop, watch whatever sporting event might be showing on the TV screens over the bar, or just gaze at those gorgeous bartenders and wish one of them would take a turn on the runway.

THE LIBRARY
3785 Boulder Hwy., Las Vegas (#10 on map, pg. 39)

Phone: (702) 641-6800
Hours: Sun.–Wed. 5 p.m.–4 a.m., Thurs.–Sat. 1 p.m.–6 a.m.
Minimum Age: 21
Valet Parking: No; located on well-lit busy street
Cover Charge: Non-locals, $10; locals, $5; ladies, free; unlimited lifetime pass, $25
Full Bar: Yes
Food: No
Lap Dances: Main room, $20; VIP room, half-hour/$200
Website: librarytoplesslv.com

Grade of Club: B
Grade of Dancer: Mostly fine and average, some very fine, some below average
SPW: 55%

Snyder Says: Try tipping the club's plumber
to turn up the water pressure.

Let me direct your attention to that SPW rating of 55%, the second-highest SPW of any topless club in Vegas. What makes this club so special?

The shower.

A Plexiglas-enclosed shower is installed behind the bar and once every hour or so, one of the dancers does a two-song set inside. The three showerheads ensure that she gets really drenched and it's very well-lit. Even better, if the elastic on her panties isn't tight, she spends a lot of time trying to keep them from sliding off in the spray. It's a real battle between a sweet young girl and three powerful determined showerheads, and believe me, every guy in the joint is rooting for the showerheads to win. So many times, those panties will come down right to the brink of heaven, she'll give the waistband a quick yank, and your stopped heart will start beating again. As strip-club shows go, this one is hot, and it's definitely worth checking out even if you've never before ventured to the east side of town. The shower show is performed only when the club is crowded, so don't expect to see it on most week nights. Come on Friday and Saturday nights when they turn on the water. The best seats for these shows are the barstools.

The dancers here are a mix of hot and sexy babes who could work in any of the top clubs if they wanted to (some of them do on other nights) and second-rate dancers, just local girls with a little too much body fat to work in the top clubs. If you like chunkier girls, you can always count on finding a few here.

The high-end dancers work here for the more relaxed atmosphere. This isn't a club where girls are continually hustling drinks and lap dances. They don't have to, because the club fees are low. According to one dancer, they get to keep all the money they make from lap and VIP-room dances, except for a 10% tipout at the end of their shift.

The "Gold Card" Perks

The Library is a true locals strip club—a blue-collar joint for the regular Joes in Henderson. The real regulars pay $25 for a "Gold Card" that allows them free admission for life. If you don't have a Gold Card, admission is still only $5. A beer here is $6, though on weekends the DJ announces drink specials throughout the night, sometimes for Gold Card holders only, sometimes just for the guys who tip the girl getting wet.

In addition to the shower, the main stage has two poles and is big enough for the better dancers to show their moves; the smaller stage, with a single pole, is up against the back wall, used only when the club is crowded.

Lap dances here are $20, performed only in booths along the side walls. Don't expect high-mileage laps. There is also a VIP room where you can go with the dancer of your choice for $200 for a half-hour. The VIP room gets so little use that you'll likely be alone with a dancer there, and no bouncer stands at the door watching you.

A pool room with two tables gets used a lot on the weekends and strategically located video screens show sporting events. Despite the great shower shows and the better-than-average stage shows, this club is rarely crowded, even on weekends.

To sum up, the Library is a little undiscovered gem on the east side of town. This is one of only two topless joints in Vegas to get an SPW rating better than 50%, and that's because I like to see dancers get wet.

OG
(formerly Olympic Garden)
1531 Las Vegas Blvd. S., Las Vegas (#11 on map, pg. 39)

Phone: (702) 385-8987
Hours: 24/7
Minimum Age: 21
Valet Parking: Yes; well-lit lot on heavily trafficked street
Cover Charge: After 6 p.m. $30; locals, $10 if arriving in own vehicle
Full Bar: Yes
Food: Yes; pizza, sandwiches, etc., ordered from nearby restaurants
Lap Dances: Main room, $20; VIP room, 3 songs/$100 + $40 bar tab, half-hour/$300 + $80 bar tab
Website: ogvegas.com

Grade of Club: A
Grade of Dancer: Mostly fine and average, some very fine, some below average
SPW: 50%

Snyder Says: Oh gee! Only g-strings!

There once was a time—not too many years ago—when this club ruled the Vegas gentlemen's-club scene. Every night it was packed to the rafters. It was big on tits, and any dancer who didn't have natural bigguns had a boob job. All the dancers were young and beautiful with not an ounce of fat on them.

But OG has lost its premier standing. It still draws a pretty good crowd on weekends, but it's not what it used to be. I think what's happened is the local guys have defected to Sapphire, Spearmint Rhino, Cheetahs, Badda Bing, Seamless, and Treasures, among others. Every one of these other clubs has a locals free-admission policy, whereas OG charges locals $10 to get in. The cost of a half-hour in the VIP room in any of these other clubs, including the bar tab where applicable, is between $240 and $280. The cost of a half-hour in OG's VIP room, including the bar tab, is $380. That's a big difference and locals tend to notice these things when they go from club to club. So OG has turned into much more of a club for tourists who don't know standard Vegas prices.

On Friday and Saturday nights, however, this place really rocks. When the town is bulging with tourists, the visitors always find OG; it's the only major topless club located right on the Strip. And lots of gorgeous dancers show up to work the weekend crowds here.

There are two rooms, plus the VIP room. There's not much in the way of stage lighting, but the general lighting inside the place is better than most clubs. They've got the requisite flashing blues and reds, but the club has less of that dark/flashing look than most of the high-tech clubs. As in most of the Vegas topless clubs, the VIP room isn't all that private.

OG is one of the topless clubs in town where you can come just to relax and watch the dancers on stage. The rail seats are popular and the stage dancers really pay attention to the tippers. You don't need to get a lap dance or go into the VIP room to have fun.

PLAY IT AGAIN SAM
4120 W. Spring Mountain Rd., Las Vegas (#13 on map, pg. 39)

Phone: (702) 876-1550
Hours: 24/7
Minimum Age: 21
Valet Parking: No; well-lit lot on heavily trafficked street
Cover Charge: Two drink minimum ($10 after 8 p.m. for non-locals Fri. and Sat.)
Full Bar: Yes
Food: Yes; 11 a.m.–3 a.m. daily
Lap Dances: Main room, $20; VIP room, half-hour/$100, includes a bottle of champagne
Website: playitagainsams.com

Grade of Club: B
Grade of Dancer: Mostly average and below average, a couple fine or very fine
SPW: 15%

Snyder Says: Best VIP deal in town …
if you can find a dancer …

Play It Again Sam is a locals joint. I don't quite get the Bogart theme, but then again ... Why not?

This club has the best VIP-room deal in town. A half-hour with a dancer in the Fantasy Room is only $100 and includes a bottle of champagne! Obviously, it won't be Dom, but Sam's price undercuts the competition by a large margin. The Fantasy Room is big, with dim lighting and a dozen booths, not a whole lot different from other VIP rooms in this town.

I must admit, however, that I haven't tried the VIP room here, even though I've often seen dancers I'd go in with. But none of them have ever approached me. Dancers in the high-end clubs always seem to be on the hunt, relentlessly hustling laps and private dances, while dancers in the locals clubs tend to sit around drinking with people they already know when they're not on stage And it doesn't make any difference if you sit on the rail and tip the dancers you like in the locals clubs. You still won't be approached. This is one of the main problems in the locals clubs for shy guys. The dancers know each other and the regular customers, while outsiders and newcomers are often ignored. So if you see a dancer you like here, you'll have to be pretty aggressive to get that great VIP-room deal.

Play It Again Sam has a pretty big stage and the lighting is dim, but not bad. The dancers respond to tips while they're on stage. They run the gamut from below average to fine, but below average to average is the norm. This is another place for men who prefer plumper women, but you occasionally see high-end dancers who like the more relaxed non-hustle atmosphere.

With most of the major topless clubs charging $7 to $9 for a domestic beer, it's nice that Sam's keeps its evening price at $5.25. The afternoon price is $3.50 and dancers are usually here then too. The club also offers 25¢ bartop video poker machines and video poker players drink for free.

Sam's has their own kitchen and takes pride in their food. It's mostly simple stuff—burgers, sandwiches, fries, salads, etc., but they also cook up complete breakfasts, with most items priced in the $5–$8 range. The sandwiches are big and come with fries.

RICK'S CABARET
(formerly SCORES, formerly Jaguars)
3355 Procyon St., Las Vegas (#14 on map, pg. 39)

Phone: (702) 367-4000
Hours: 4 p.m.–8 a.m.
Minimum Age: 21
Valet Parking: Yes; well-lit lot, doorman always out front
Cover Charge: $30; locals, free if arriving in own vehicle
Full Bar: Yes
Food: Yes
Lap Dances: Main room, $20; VIP room, 3 songs/$100 + 2 drinks, half-hour/$200 + bar tab, full hour/$400 + bar tab; see description
Website: ricks.com

Grade of Club: A
Grade of Dancer: Mostly fine and very fine, some average
SPW: 55%

Snyder Says: A sizzling stage show
and striptease lap dances!

Over the past few years operating as SCORES, this club became something of a locals' favorite, primarily because of a great VIP club. In September 2008, it changed ownership and is now Rick's Cabaret. Locals with a SCORES VIP card can trade it in for a Rick's VIP card or just show the cashier a Nevada driver's license. The free card allows locals to get all domestic beers and well drinks for $5 each and that's every day of the week, 24/7.

For the first few months of operation as Rick's, the stage in this club had no stripper pole, so the dancers compensated by concentrating on floor work. Most topless clubs put the dancers on postage-stamp-sized stages with the dimmest possible lighting and just tell them to wiggle around. But at Rick's, with a bigger stage and no pole, the dancers provided a great show just by rolling around the floor in their g-strings. Whew! The dancers were making scads of tip money from the rail, even though multiple girls were on the stage simultaneously. It was definitely the sexiest stage show of any topless club in town.

Rick's finished the remodel and the stage now has a stripper pole, but thankfully, the pole is located toward the back of the stage and the dancers seem to have gotten used to doing lots of floor work, so the show has remained one of the best stage shows you'll see in a Vegas topless joint, and there are still usually multiple dancers on stage at once. So Rick's gets one of the highest SPW ratings of any topless club in town.

Rick's lavish interior is the setting for the city's "hottest stage show."

How About a "Lap Strip?"

But it gets even better. I've also noticed something else unusual about this club. Among the hundred or so dancers working the floor, many of those who aren't actually in a guy's lap are walking around in *dresses*. Some are wearing long, slinky, satin gowns; others are in revealing lacy numbers that allow you to see their Victoria's Secret ensembles beneath; some wear tight little mini-dresses that come down to the tops of their stockings so you can see that sexy flash of white thigh when they walk by.

In every other topless joint, most dancers work the floor in skimpy tops and g-strings or bikini panties, rarely dresses. Semi-formal wear not only makes the club look much more elegant, but what's really great is that if you spring for a lap dance, you get to help the dancer peel her dress off. A striptease in your lap? Stop my heart!

Close to the club entrance is a room called the Piano Bar, though I've never seen anyone playing a piano in there. All the seats, other than those at the bar, are for guys who order expensive booze by the bottle. Despite the small mini-stage in this room with a stripper pole, the Piano Bar is primarily for guys who want lap dances with bottle service. If that's not you, don't waste your time in there. Bottle prices

Rick's SPW of 55% is one of Vegas' highest!

start at $250 for a Moet & Chandon champagne and go up to well over $1,000 for the premium bubbles.

The three VIP rooms are up a winding staircase on the second floor—one for the guys who pay $100 for three dances, one for the guys who pay $200 for a half-hour, and a more private one for the guys who pay $400 for a full hour. The required bar tab for the $100 room is two drinks, and bar tabs for the more expensive VIPs range from $75 to $150, depending which room you choose. None are one-on-one rooms, but they're all dark and intimate and comfortable.

Food service is available throughout business hours. The eating area is on a level above the main floor and offers an excellent view of the stage, so you can watch the dancers while you eat. The menu is extensive with lots of gourmet items, all reasonably priced. I tried the seared ahi tuna with jalapeño and Mandarin oranges with a baby bok choy salad and it was delicious. Price: $24. Most dinners are priced from $23 to $25 and the choices include seafood, poultry, and grilled specialties. Service is attentive and reasonably fast.

SAPPHIRE
3025 Industrial Rd., Las Vegas (#15 on map, pg. 39)

Phone: (702) 796-6000
Hours: 24/7
Minimum Age: 21
Valet Parking: Yes; lot is well-lit with attendants
Cover Charge: $30; locals, free if arriving in own vehicle; no cover 6 a.m.–6 p.m.
Full Bar: Yes
Food: Yes
Lap Dances: Main room, $20; VIP room, 3 songs/$100 + 2 drinks, half-hour/$200 + 4 drinks, full hour/$400 + $300 bar tab
Website: sapphirelasvegas.com

Grade of Club: A
Grade of Dancer: Mostly fine and very fine, some average
SPW: 45%

Snyder Says: Sapphire is the biggest
and determined to be the best.

At Sapphire's first Monday Night Football bash of the 2008 season, I could hardly believe the spread: Buffet tables were set up in both the main room and the big downstairs VIP room groaned with food cooked by local restaurants. Layalina Mediterranean had a set-up, as did La Focaccia Italian and Stripburgers. In addition to typical bar-food items like hot dogs, hamburgers, pizza, etc., there were great pasta dishes, Mediterranean wraps, and a whole table of Mexican food. How much did they charge, you ask? How about free! And not only that, there was free booze! The party was sponsored by Heineken and Stoli Vodka, so young lovelies were standing all around the club with tubs full of Heineken on ice and bottles of Stoli for shots or mixed drinks, and it was all gratis from 4 p.m. until 8 p.m.

I have no idea what that kickoff party cost the club, but there must have been 1,000 guys there drinking and eating with a vengeance for four straight hours. Plus, at half-time, there were $1 lap dances from the hundreds of babes roaming the aisles with nothing to do but find a guy waving a buck in the air to signal he wanted a quickie before the second half started. Sapphire knows how to throw a party.

After that first MNF blowout, Sapphire reined it in a bit and for the MNF parties for the rest of the season, they charged all attendees a flat $20 admission. Still, the charge covered three drinks and all the food you could eat from a Milano's Pizza buffet. They still had the dollar lap dances during half-time and a huge crowd; everyone who was there the first week saw what a great party it was. It's also a great club for watching a football game, with multiple huge flat-screen TV monitors and a terrific sound system.

If you're just vacationing in Las Vegas, you may not be here on a Monday night during football season. But you should check out Sapphire anyway. The reason I started this review with the MNF party is to show you how determined this place is to be not only the biggest strip club in town, but also the best.

Sapphire advertises itself as the "World's Largest Gentlemen's Club," and I suspect it may be. When this club first opened in 2002, I wondered if it would survive. For the first few years, it appeared to be struggling, and the problem seemed to be that it was just too big. When you walked into the 10,000-square-foot main showroom, if it had 100 customers, it appeared nearly empty. Also, Sapphire was charging locals a $10 admission fee, unlike the other major topless clubs in town where locals are admitted free. By 2005, rumor had it that the club was going to be razed to build a high-rise.

In 2006, however, one of the co-owners, who didn't want to see the club die, bought the whole thing for $80 million. Since then, the club has flourished. The new owner has made the exact changes the club needed, including ending the practice of charging the locals an admission fee.

To deal with the problem of the club's size, Sapphire started using a huge floor-to-ceiling curtain to cut the main showroom in half during less-than-peak hours. Even when this curtain is closed, the club looks bigger than most other strip clubs, but now, it doesn't look empty even when there's a good-sized crowd in the place. This curtain also

Sapphire is huge—"The biggest strip club in the world."

squeezes the dancers working the floor into a tighter space, which increases the impression of a wealth of available female flesh—a definite improvement.

Still, as gentlemen's clubs go, this place is huge, with three full bars and three stages for dancers. The center stage is on a platform about 20 feet up, so this dancer is mostly on her own up there. If you want to watch her, either rent a skybox or bring your binoculars. The guys on the main floor watch the dancers on the two stages at either side of the center-stage platform.

The lower stages are small, the lighting is the typical flashing reds and blues that I find so irritating, and they're elevated higher than most strip club stages, like the main stage at Club Paradise. If you, like me, prefer to sit on the rail, you're pretty much staring at the dancer's feet. The dancers try to compensate by rewarding tippers on the rail with a lot of extra attention, often coming over the rail to tease the boys.

The silicone factor in this club is high. If you like big tits, you'll like a lot of these dancers, most of whom are on the high end of the spectrum for both beauty and body.

As this is primarily a lap-dance club, it is suitably dark, and even when there's a big crowd, plenty of dancers are working the crowd. The lap dances on the main floor are relatively high-contact, priced at $20 per song like everywhere else. The dancers in this place work the crowd relentlessly when they're not on stage, but with so many guys, no one tries to hard-sell a dance. If you politely turn down a dancer, she'll quickly move on.

The VIP rooms are also priced in and around the industry standard: a half-hour for $200 or a full hour for $400. Add a bar-tab requirement for the VIP rooms.

Stripper Karaoke

Sapphire also offers a karaoke room—one of the most unusual VIPs I've seen anywhere. It's a fairly large room with a small stage and a top-of-the-line karaoke system, with some 70,000 song selections, three microphones, comfortable seating for up to 40 people, and a stripper pole right in the middle of the room. You can bring dancers here for $400 per hour for each dancer, and if you're with your buddies, up to three of you can split the $300 bar tab. The VIP-room host tells me it's not uncommon for a group of guys to rent the room for an hour, then end up staying two or three hours because they're having so much fun.

Unfortunately, you can't watch the nuttiness in the karaoke room if you're not with a dancer and paying her hourly fee. I wish they'd start up a regular once-a-week open-mike karaoke show, with both customers and strippers taking turns at the mike.

The Skyboxes

Sapphire also has 10 "skyboxes" for rent, essentially private mini-VIP rooms with multiple couches that accommodate up to a dozen people. The skyboxes are 25 feet above the main floor and have full-length windows that overlook the club below; they also have their own controls for lighting and music volume and even a flat-screen TV. Skybox rentals start at $750, not including the dancer(s).

Sapphire has no restaurant on the premises, but any cocktail waitress will take an order for Fatburgers and bring you your food in a reasonable amount of time. Fatburgers is a national chain; in addition to regular hamburgers, the menu includes chicken burgers, turkey burgers, and veggie burgers, with the standard sides like fries, rings, chili, shakes, etc. Heart-attack food.

> Sapphire takes the prize for "best lap dances" and "most unconventional VIP room" with its stripper karaoke.

Rockin' top and bottom at Sapphire

Sapphire's skyboxes accommodate up to a dozen partiers (split the tab and it's not too bad).

I wouldn't come here to drink, because $12 for a domestic bottle of beer is quite a bit steeper than the other major topless clubs. I also wouldn't come here if I just wanted to watch dancers. The nude clubs have much better stage shows, and if you want to drink and watch, many topless clubs have better stages and lower-priced drinks.

As a local, I go to this club for special events like Monday Night Football, or for a lap or VIP-room dance, which are priced competitively and the selection of dancers here is always great. It's fun to have such a wide range of choices.

And Sapphire is the first strip club to forge a full-fledged partnership with a casino, by way of the Rio's summertime pool party—it's stocked with Sapphire girls all summer long (see "Topless Pools").

SEAMLESS
4740 S. Arville St., Las Vegas (#16 on map, pg. 39)

Phone: (702) 227-5200
Hours: 24/7
Minimum Age: 21
Valet Parking: Yes; well-lit lot with attendants outside
Cover Charge: Non-locals, $20 after 8 p.m.; locals, free
Full Bar: Yes
Food: No
Lap Dances: Main room, $20; VIP room, 3 songs/$100, half-hour/ $200 + $40 bar tab
Website: seamlessclub.com

Grade of Club: A
Grade of Dancer: Mostly fine and very fine, some average
SPW: 50%

Snyder Says: Twenty-first-century taxi dancing!

Seamless doesn't seem to know whether it wants to be a strip club or a nightclub. So it tries to be both and crazy as it sounds, it appears to be succeeding. In fact, this place seems to have become a new kind of strip club.

Every night at 4 a.m. they stop featuring strippers on the main stage and start playing dance music for the after-hours nightclubbers. A couple of go-go dancers in bikini outfits dance at the corners of the center bar, but the topless show in the main room is over. Some of the tables go up onto the stage and others are cleared away to create a dance floor. Seamless advertises its DJs in the *Las Vegas Weekly* and on its website, and the special events are geared toward a mixed audience. For example, Monday is Ladies Night with complimentary champagne from 4 a.m. to 6 a.m.

My understanding of the way this was supposed to work was the VIP rooms would stay open after 4 a.m. for guys who wanted to keep playing around with the topless dancers, while the main room would become a club for a mixed crowd that wanted to party after hours.

What actually happened, however, was that the VIP rooms filled up with the dancers, while most of the guys in the club for the topless show stayed in the main room and kept drinking. Some after-hours clubbers showed up, but not that many. The main room ended up having a huge ratio of men to women, while the VIP rooms had a huge ratio of dancers to men.

The Return of Taxi Dancing—With a Twist

So Seamless management gave the dancers permission to start trolling the main room for customers to bring into the VIP. A wise decision. Now what you've got is a nightclub scene with a hundred babes in sexy lingerie mixed in with a few after-hours clubgoers and the guys who were there initially. Some guys buy drinks for the dancers. Some ask the dancers if they want to get out on the dance floor and boogie, and some of the dancers do. Some take up the dancers on their invitations to retire to the VIP room. It's turned into a scene where a guy can actually socialize with a dancer in a nightclub setting before going into the VIP room for a private show/lap dance.

They say many of the best inventions are accidents, of which Seamless is a great example. This unusual and cool strip club is halfway between a modern strip club and those old "taxi-dancing" clubs from the 1920s and '30s, where guys went into what seemed like a dance hall filled with beautiful women and danced with the ladies for a dime a dance. Of course, the only thing available back then was some dancing and conversation. It was a dating fantasy for lonely men. Now, instead of paying the girl a dime, you buy her a drink, boogie with her awhile, then go undress her in the VIP. The old dating fantasy club has returned with a potent modern twist.

For a lot of guys, I think it's more fun to pick a girl out of a crowd in a nightclub setting before taking her into the VIP room. Guys get to feel more like they're on the hunt, rather than getting hustled.

Adding to the weirdness of this after-hours ultralounge is the fact that the main room has comfortable seating areas with couches and tables along the walls reserved for guests who pay for bottle service. High rollers take advantage of these furniture arrangements by ordering a bottle during strip-club hours, then using the area as a lair to attract lap dancers. So, although topless girls are no longer on the main stage or lap dancing in the free seating areas, some are still doing laps for the guys with reserved seats out in the main room.

The most amusing thing about this club after 4 a.m. is the accidental tourist. Some rube from who knows where stumbles in, but has no idea what this joint is. I don't know how, but out-of-place visitors eventually manage to find every nook and cranny of this town. You see them in the strip clubs all the time—some middle-aged couple from Idaho that looks so lost and confused. But how do they wind up at Seamless at 5 a.m.? Is this some sadistic cabbie's idea of a joke?

It's Saturday night, or should I say early Sunday morning. Two married couples enter the club together. Hopefully, they aren't looking for church services. Maybe the husbands are insurance agents, in town for a convention or something. You can tell this is their big night out on the town, because they're wearing their snazzy suits and their wives are dolled up, earrings and everything. The four of them huddle together just inside the main-room entrance for mutual support and protection. I mean, geez, black dudes are walking around with pierced eyelids! So the four of them are scanning the premises for someplace to sit down and maybe have a cocktail before getting a cab back to their rooms at Excalibur. But there's no place to sit down.

And although this place looks like a nightclub and people are drinking and dancing, many of the women are walking around in their underwear—little lacy bra-and-panty sets with fuck-me platform heels. And everyone's acting like that's completely normal! The insurance guys keep elbowing each other. Look at her! Look at her! But their wives are gritting their teeth and steaming. What the hell is this place?

Then they spy some empty upholstered chairs against the far wall. They don't know these seats are reserved and they won't be allowed to sit there, so they start winding their way through the crowd toward the seats … But they stop in their tracks when they see a guy sitting on the couch next to the seats they were hoping to claim, with a girl wearing nothing but a g-string straddling him with her tits in his face.

Of course, not one of them has ever seen a lap dance before. They don't know what a lap dance is. All they know is WE GOTTA GET THE HELL OUTTA HERE!

Before the witching hour of 4 a.m. when Seamless is just a strip

club, the look is standard high-tech. The main stage has decent lighting for dancers and they're so good-looking they make you glad they're well-lit. But sitting on the rail is unfortunately painful, because of the sound system. The woofers are located right at stage

Be careful you don't get lost in Seamless' many-mirrored maze-like restrooms.

front, with the bass cranked up so loud that it makes your molars hurt. But if you think the rail seats are empty, think again. A lot of guys put up with blasted eardrums to get close to the dancers, who do a good show.

Lap dances out on the main floor are $20. Higher-mileage dances take place in the two VIP rooms. One room is for customers who want three songs for $100. The other is for customers willing to pay $200 for a half-hour, plus a $40 bar tab. This VIP room is a bit more private and a little more plush.

Anyway, my compliments to whoever dreamed up this after-hours concept. But do me a favor and turn the fucking bass down a few decibels when the topless dancers are on stage. I'd like to sit on the rail without stuffing cotton in my ears.

Seamless Players Card

You can get a Seamless Players Card free from the front cashier by showing an ID that verifies you're 21 or over. Each time you enter the club, one "credit point" is added to your SPC account. Points are currently valued at $1 each in trade for Seamless good or services. For example, with 20 points, you can get a lap dance. Other member benefits—such as reduced prices on bottles—aren't tied to points.

SPEARMINT RHINO
3340 S. Highland Dr., Las Vegas (#17 on map, pg. 39)

Phone: (702) 796-3600
Hours: 24/7
Minimum Age: 21
Valet Parking: Yes; well-lit lot with attendants and usually waiting cabs
Cover Charge: $30; locals, free if arriving in own vehicle
Full Bar: Yes
Food: Yes
Lap Dances: Main room, $20; VIP room, 3 songs/$100, half-hour/$200 + 2 drinks, full hour/$400 + 4 drinks; Private booth, full hour/$400 + $375 bottle
Website: spearmintrhino.com

Grade of Club: A
Grade of Dancer: Mostly fine and very fine, some average
SPW: 50%

Snyder Says: Drop-dead gorgeous dancers
and high-mileage laps.

The Rhino is one of the plushest clubs in Vegas, having eschewed the typical high-tech look for something more opulent and flattering to skin tones. Think English country manor with lots of comfy seating, fake paintings (nudes, of course), muted lighting, big ceramic vases in the passageways, and so many dancers that no matter where you sit or stand in this place, you're within three feet of a babe with long legs, big tits, and a smile. A sign inside the entrance says, "Maximum Occupancy: 999," and I suspect that they often approach the max. I'm always amazed that there seem to be as many dancers as customers.

There's one main and two smaller stages, but this is primarily a lap-dance club. It's appropriately dark out on the floor. If your opinion of flashing lights and high-tech decor is anything like mine, you'll find Spearmint Rhino a welcome relief.

The VIP rooms are small spaces with multiple booths. On many

nights, you'll have to wait for a booth to become available as they're almost always all in use. There are separate VIP rooms for the hour, half-hour dances, and three-song dances. The hour-long room is more elegant with comfier roomier couches, though it's not any more private. If you want a real private space with a dancer, the only such booth in the club is often available, as you must pay the $375 bottle fee in addition to the $400 charge for the dancer's time

It's All About Comfort

There's no pressure to buy anything here. You can look at the girls all you want and no one gives a damn if you're drinking or not. Dancers approach you to see if you're interested in having some fun, but they don't pressure you if you're not. If you haven't been here before and you're considering something more than a lap dance out on the main floor, I suggest you ask a dancer to give you a tour of the different rooms. You'll probably note that the degree of physical contact is a lot higher in the VIP rooms than out on the main floor.

This place gets packed just about every night of the week. The locals like it, the tourists like it, the high rollers like it. For a club this big and with this many drop-dead-gorgeous dancers, it has a comfortable homey feeling. The dancers are making good money, the bar's making money, the club's raking in shitloads. If it ain't broke, don't fix it.

The Rhino serves food 24 hours a day (except for Sunday, the cook's day off). The selection of breakfast, lunch, and dinner items includes steak and eggs for $10; most sandwiches, salads, etc. are in the $6–$10 range. The happy-hour food specials (1–4 p.m.) are a good deal—for example, a burger, fries, and beer for $5. You probably won't see many (if any) stage dancers at this early time of day, except a few sitting around to see if any guys are ready for a lap or VIP dance.

The Rhino is heavily supported by the locals, including me. Expect great food and drink deals, friendly staff, and good-looking dancers who never make you feel you're being hustled.

TREASURES

2801 Westwood Dr., Las Vegas (#19 on map, pg. 39)

Phone: (702) 257-3030
Hours: Sun.–Thurs. 4 p.m.–6 a.m., Fri. and Sat. 4 p.m.–8 a.m.
Minimum Age: 21
Valet Parking: Yes; well-lit fenced private lot
Cover Charge: $30; locals, free
Full Bar: Yes
Food: Steakhouse
Lap Dances: Main room, $20; VIP room, 3 songs/$100 + 2 drinks, half-hour/$250 + 2 drinks, full hour/$500 + 4 drinks. Private VIP room, half-hour/$250 + $125 bar tab, full hour/$500 + $250 bar tab
Website: treasureslasvegas.com

Grade of Club: A
Grade of Dancer: Mostly fine and very fine, some average
SPW: 50%

Snyder Says: The dinner fantasy done right.

Treasures is unique among the Vegas gentlemen's clubs: It has a small gourmet steakhouse where customers can invite dancers from the club to dine with them. If having an elegant dinner date with a hot babe appeals to you, this is the place. Why would you want to pay for a stripper's dinner? Hey, think of it. She'll wear something sexy, but more modest than she'd wear out in the main room of the club. You get to sit and flirt with each other for a nice leisurely hour while you dine. Then you can take her into the VIP room and undress her and ravish her—at least to the extent that she allows ravishing. The two hours will run you about $1,000 total. I can think of worse ways to blow a thousand bucks in Vegas in two hours (craps, roulette, baccarat ...).

How's the food? There's definitely a real chef in the kitchen, so it's on a par with the average Las Vegas casino steakhouse, which tends to be pretty good. Just don't expect the quality of Delmonico's at Venetian or Craftsteak at MGM Grand. It's on the pricey side, but not bad if you like steakhouse fare. Entrée prices range from $32 for a mini-filet to $65 for surf and turf. Everything on the menu is a la carte, so expect to pay $50 to $100 per person for dinner and more if you have wine or cocktails with your meal. I had the mini-filet and it was a good cut of meat. The French onion soup was a bit heavy on the cheese. The asparagus was lightly cooked, California style, with an excellent Hollandaise.

An Ambience of Money

Treasures is designed to cater to a well-heeled clientele. It's an opulent mansion-style gentlemen's club, sort of a cross between the Italian villa look of Rick's Cabaret and the imperial Roman look of Caesars Palace. The dripping-with-wealth theme continues on the inside, with a winding staircase and balconies and drapes, a swank joint where Hefner would surely feel at home.

The good-looking dancers are mostly fine and very fine and the center stage is excellent for watching them. It's big enough for a dancer to move and it's low enough for her to get down close to the customers sitting on the rail. During slow periods, only the center stage is used,

"If having an elegant dinner date with a hot babe appeals to you, Treasures is the place."

which is good, because the main stage is not nearly as customer friendly.

I'm not crazy about the main-stage stripper pole, a very bright tube light that alternates in color between red and blue. Trying to watch a dancer on that stage gives you a headache. Just sit on the rail at the center stage if you're there to watch the dancers.

Lighting in the club is on the dark side, fine for a lap-dance club. There's also a more private VIP area (smaller and darker), where the price for the dancer is the same, but you'll have a bigger bar tab—$125 for a half-hour or $250 for an hour. If you're with a buddy and you each want to take a girl into this room, they'll allow you to split the bar tab. If you're with a dancer you just had dinner with, you'll likely have this VIP room to yourself, especially if it's not too late in the evening.

Finally, Treasures has one of the best ongoing happy hours in town (in or out of the strip clubs). Well drinks and domestic beers are free from 4 to 6 pm every day, and all drinks are 2-for-1 from 4 till 8. A good free buffet is also served from 4 till 8.

VELVET LION
(formerly Eden, formerly Striptease)
3750 S. Valley View Blvd., Las Vegas (#20 on map, pg. 39)

Phone: (702) 253-1555
Hours: 8 p.m.–6 a.m. daily
Minimum Age: 21
Valet Parking: Yes; well-lit fenced private lot
Cover Charge: $30; locals, free
Full Bar: Yes
Food: No
Lap Dances: Main room, $20, 3 songs/$100; VIP room, half-hour/ $200 + 2 drinks, full hour/$400 + 4 drinks; Champagne room, full hour/$400 + premium bottle ($275 min.); Celebrity room, full hour/ $400 + $500 bottle min.
Website: velvetlion.com

Grade of Club: A
Grade of Dancer: Mostly fine and very fine, some average
SPW: 50%

Snyder Says: The snake is gone
and the cat's out of the bag.

119

"Robin Leach is inda house! Robin Leach is inda house!"

It was the first time I'd ever heard that announcement in a strip joint. Robin Leach? Does he have a new show in the works? "Lifestyles of the Rich and Horny?"

"Nick Nolte is onda way! Nick Nolte is onda way!"

My heart is going pitter-pat. Wow. Nick Nolte! It's opening night at the Velvet Lion and the DJ can hardly contain himself. "Fifty Cent is inda house! Fifty Cent!"

For many years, this club was a low-end dive called Striptease. It was renovated in 2007 and turned into a dark and comfy lap dance palace, renamed Eden. Eden's most memorable feature was a huge boa constrictor that lived in a Plexiglas enclosure just inside the entrance. Eden struggled for more than a year to find a clientele that never materialized. Then came another change of ownership, another renovation, and the club reopened in December 2008 as the Velvet Lion.

I was surprised to hear that the new owners were renovating a club that had just been renovated. I liked Eden's interior design, which featured a two-level stage with red tube lighting around the base to illuminate the dancers. It was much easier on the eyes than the flashing reds and blues used by so many topless joints, and lighting the dancers from the lower inside perimeter of the stage also provided an excellent view to the guys sitting on the rail. Eden's main room was the darkest room in Vegas, even darker than Cheetahs, and darkness is generally a plus for the lap-dance crowd. Given its prime location, I'm not sure why the club never attracted bigger crowds. Perhaps it was that godawful serpent that was there to play up the "Eden" theme. As snakes go, it was a big one. They fed it every Sunday—a rabbit. But for whatever reason Eden couldn't attract customers, the dancer quality deteriorated as time went on (more hefty older dancers and fewer in the fine to very fine category), and low-end dancers will ultimately put any strip club on life support in a town like Vegas where the competition is so tough.

Velvet Lion had more customers on opening night than Eden had been seeing in a typical month. The place was packed. The remodel was extensive. The faux-tiger-skin carpeting was a nice touch, as were the go-go dancers in g-strings with their bodies painted like tigers and leopards. The club now has two bars and two small, low, one-pole stages with the typical red-and-blue flashers. Other lighting includes a big crystal chandelier in the front room, making the whole place more well-lit than Eden ever was. But despite those flashing lights, which I'm not crazy about, I must admit the stage heights are perfect for watching dancers close up, with lots of rail seats at both stages.

The main thing Velvet Lion has, however, that Eden never had is a lot of dancers on the higher end of the body spectrum. This club is big on tits—lots of boob jobs—so if you're a tit man, you'll definitely like this place.

As per the data box, you'll find the lap-dance and VIP-room costs to be typical for Vegas topless clubs, and with domestic beers at $6, they're pricing themselves into the market. The VIP room is fairly large, with lots of comfortable booths. The champagne room is a smaller room inside the VIP area, with diaphanous curtains that can be closed around the individual couches to give customers even more privacy. The celebrity room is the most private walled-off area at the front of

the VIP room, where the "celebrities" and their dancers sit behind a one-way mirror, through which they can view the club, but cannot be seen. A separate room, with smaller booths, accommodates guys who want three dances for $100.

I attended both the "soft" opening and the grand opening a few weeks later, and both nights the place was packed. I

Reviewing the Topless Clubs

observed very little lap-dance activity in the main rooms and the VIP rooms were also not much in use. And despite the crowds and the abundance of rail seats at both stages, there just wasn't much tipping of the stage dancers. Lots of gorgeous babes, but not much happening for them in the tipping department. I do think the brighter lighting discourages some customers from getting lap dances, but it struck me that it may also have been just the opening-night scene itself. Would you want to get a lap dance with Robin Leach and Nick Nolte staring at you? But I also got a feeling that these crowds weren't so much strip-club crowds as nightclub crowds and I wondered how the club would fare after the razzle-dazzle opening.

A few weeks later I went back to the Velvet Lion at midnight on a Friday when Sapphire, Cheetahs, and the Rhino were all going gang-busters. As I suspected, the Lion's crowd was sparse in comparison. The back room was all but empty and there were more dancers than customers in the front room. The dancers themselves are all gorgeous, so from the customers' perspective, this is a great scene. If you sit on the rail, you'll get a lot of attention from the stage dancers, and you've got a fantastic selection of top-end dancers for the VIP rooms, where you'll have more privacy than you'd ever imagine in the more popular joints.

But if the nightclub crowds have all gone back to Pure and Tao and Body English, and Velvet Lion can't get the guys from the strip joints to leave their favorite haunts and check them out, those high-end dancers will all disappear back to the top clubs where they can make money.

It's hard to tell what's going to happen with a new club. I'll keep an eye on the Lion, as I suspect it'll be going through changes for the first six months or so. It's obvious that a strong creative team is behind this joint, with a marketing genius at the helm. Maybe he can make it happen. I was amazed to see this dead zone—formerly Eden, and Striptease before that—with standing room only on opening night, and in mid-December at that.

8

Reviewing the Nude Clubs

In the following pages, you'll find reviews of all of Las Vegas' nude clubs, arranged alphabetically. Each includes a data box at the top with pertinent information about location and hours, a photograph of the club's exterior, and the three ratings discussed in Chapter 7: Grade of Club, Grade of Dancer, and SPW. All nude clubs are rated either Grade A or Grade D, and there ain't no in between. A Grade D club is not a club with low-end dancers, but a club that's *not a regular strip club*. Here, the stage show is of minor importance, as the emphasis is on getting you into the VIP room. My advice is to avoid Grade D clubs if you simply want to watch dancers on stage. The Grade A clubs provide much better stage shows.

Read the body of each review to get the inside scoop on prices, special events, and first-hand accounts and descriptions gathered during my multiple visits to the club.

Other than for the Palomino, none of the nude clubs in Las Vegas serve liquor, so you can go into these clubs provided you have ID that verifies you're 18 or older. You must be 21 to get into the Palomino Club.

BABES
(formerly Baby Dolls)
5901 Emerald Ave., Las Vegas (#21 on map, pg. 39)

Phone: (702) 435-7545
Hours: 3 p.m.–4 a.m.
Minimum Age: 18
Valet Parking: No; fenced well-lit private lot in warehouse district
Cover Charge: $20; locals, $10 includes two soft drinks
Full Bar: No alcohol served, soft drinks only
Food: Yes; snack food only
Lap Dances: Main room, $20/topless, $30/nude; VIP room, 5 songs/ $100, half-hour/$150, full hour/$250
Website: None

Grade of Club: A
Grade of Dancer: Mostly fine, some very fine, some average
SPW: 70%

Snyder Says: There's a great mini-stage
if you're willing to risk cancer.

Reviewing the Nude Clubs

This is an out-of-the-way club in the warehouse/factory hinterlands just north of Henderson, in a building that also houses an adult video/novelty store. When you first enter the club, you're greeted by a pretty young woman who introduces herself as "your host" and tells you that she can answer any questions you might have or make VIP-room arrangements with any of the dancers. Then she disappears and you probably won't see her again unless you flag her down for some reason. I come from the casino-gambling world and to me a "host" gets you comped fight tickets and makes sure your room has a Jacuzzi. I'm not sure why a guy would need a host in a strip club.

Babes has one of the larger main stages and the lighting isn't bad. Most of the dancers here are young and cute and a few have dynamite bodies. None of them can dance worth a damn, but they have most of the classic stripper moves down and lots of personality. You won't see the kind of fancy pole work you will see at Déjà Vu or Little Darlings, but most could easily work in the high-end topless clubs in a year or two when they turn 21. A few might find it easier to get work in the topless joints if they got the requisite boob job—the silicone factor at Babes is low.

The Off-Limits Mini-Stage

If you like watching nude dancers close up, the best stage is actually the mini-stage in the hookah-lounge area, cordoned off from the main floor of the club. The problem is that you won't be allowed to sit in this area unless you order a hookah. I tried sitting on the rail at the mini-stage one night when only two guys were in the lounge with a hookah and they were sitting at a table against the wall, not even watching the dancer. I was the only person in there tipping the dancer, but my "host" came in and told me I couldn't sit there unless I got a hookah. (Hookah rentals start at $12.) I told her I didn't smoke. She said, "Well, then you can't sit in this room." The room had 10 empty tables in it and a dancer on the mini-stage no one was watching but me. I told her I'd be happy to move if someone with a hookah showed up who wanted my seat. But she said, "No, you'll have to leave if you're not gonna smoke." I should mention here that you can see the dancer on the mini-stage from the main room, you just can't sit on the rail and tip her. The hookah area is not a separate room, just a roped-off area of the main room. It's not like this dancer on the mini-stage is doing a private show for the hookah crowd.

So the host in this place is kind of the opposite of what a host is in a casino. A casino host bends over backwards to make your visit a pleasure, while the Babes host's job is to be some kind of cop and enforce dumb club rules.

As in most nude clubs, lap dances don't happen out on the main floor, but in a separate side area against the wall. And like other nude clubs, this is a place where the stage dancing is the main attraction. All the dancers seem to like each other and have fun. There's almost a family kind of feel to the place.

On Wednesday nights at 11:30, the club has an "amateur contest," but don't expect to see many amateurs here. Most of the contestants appear to be professionals who pretty much put on the same show as the club's regular dancers. I suppose it's possible that some of these

contestants are amateurs, but somehow when I see a dancer in translucent platform heels, a micro-mini-skirt, a sequined thong, and pierced nipples, spinning upside down on a stripper pole, I just don't think "girl next door."

The Oil-Wrestling Show

Thursday night is oil-wrestling night with two matches—the first about 11:30 and the second an hour later. A small blow-up children's pool with an inch or so of water in front of the main stage sets the scene for the action. The

DJ attempts to auction off the rights for guys in the audience to act as "corner men" for the dancers who will be wrestling that night. He says, "We provide the lube and you rub 'em down!" He opens the bidding at $25, but if no one in the crowd puts in an opening bid, the match is delayed while the dancers go out into the crowd to find their own corner men, I suspect at a lesser price.

The nude dancer/wrestlers instruct the guys they choose as corner men that they cannot touch their breasts, buttocks, or genital areas, and the guys rub lubricant from a plastic bottle onto the dancers' shoulders and back, while the dancers rub the oil onto the more sensitive areas themselves. Then the dancers get into the pool and go at it. They wrestle for three short rounds and the crowd chooses the winner by applause at the end. The girls really wrestle and try to pin each other, so it's fun to watch.

To sum up: Let's face it, talent be damned, it's always a pleasure to watch girls get naked when they're having a good time and trying hard to put on a good show.

If Babes ever loses its "host," so I can sit on the rail (without smoking!) at the mini-stage to tip the dancers I like, I'll probably go back to this joint.

CAN CAN ROOM
3155 S. Industrial Rd., Las Vegas (#22 on map, pg. 39)

Phone: (702) 737-1161
Hours: 6 p.m.–dawn
Minimum Age: 18
Valet Parking: No; seedy neighborhood, well-lit lot attendant outside
Cover Charge: $30 + $10 drinks; locals, $10 includes two soft drinks
Full Bar: No alcohol served, soft drinks only
Food: No
Lap Dances: Negotiable, see description
Website: None

Grade of Club: D
Grade of Dancer: Mostly fine, some very fine, some average
SPW: 20%

Snyder Says: Or should it be the Can't Can't Room?

I paid my $10 locals entry fee and the cashier, a smiling lady in her sixties, told me that before I entered, she had to explain the way the Can Can Room worked, since it wasn't like the other strip clubs in Las Vegas. "Those other clubs, they have lap dancing out on the floor," she said, "but we have actual private bedrooms where you can go with the dancer of your choice."

She pulled out a colorful laminated chart about the size of a coffee-shop placemat and pointed to the options available. Option One was a half-hour in a bedroom with a dancer, listed at $350—though she was prepared to give me a deal on Option One for $100 less. Option Two provided 45 minutes in a bedroom with two dancers of my choice, while Option Three provided a full hour in a bedroom with three dancers of my choice. The list prices for these other options were higher, though both of them also had "special-deal" prices.

I asked what she meant by a bedroom. She said, "You'll have your choice of a number of different theme rooms, all of which have big comfy beds and are completely private."

"Sounds like a good deal," I said, turning to walk into the main room where the dancers were. But she stopped me and said she could come down a bit on those special-deal prices. Now, the half-hour with a single dancer that lists for $350 could be mine for just $200.

I just wanted to escape the sales pitch and get into the club. "Fantastic," I said. "I'll get back to you later. I want to go watch the dancers for a while."

Anyone vaguely familiar with the Vegas strip-club scene will recognize the famous Can Can Room sign. "That chick's in there?" No! (But the girls on the club marquees are almost always non-resident models.)

But she stopped me again and said that I could now get that half-hour for just $150, and she lowered the prices on Options Two and Three as well. "Plus," she said, "you'll get a porno video and a pen."

"A pen?" I asked.

She pulled a cheap-looking ballpoint pen from beneath the counter and held it before me in her cupped hands like it was some kind of treasure. Now, when a man is considering retiring to a bedroom for an hour with three strippers, I just don't think a ballpoint pen is going to be the deal clincher.

I told her I just wanted to watch the dancers for a while. She said, "If you don't take me up on one of the special deals I'm offering right now, I might not be able to offer those deals later. Whereas if you pay for one of the

The name Can Can Room conjures up dancers onstage, in ruffled petticoats, kicking stockinged legs over the orchestra in the pit below. But this was more like walking into the boiler room from the movie Glengarry Glen Ross.

options before you go in, you'll have five hours to choose whatever dancer or dancers you want in the bedroom."

I hadn't yet set foot into the room where the dancers were, but I was beginning to have visions of middle-aged ladies with drooping breasts and bad teeth.

Any savvy Vegas local, at this point, would have turned on his heels and made a quick exit. But as my $10 admission fee had come out of my publisher's pocket and my assignment was to get the scoop on every strip club in town, I had no choice but to soldier on.

As I turned to walk into the main room of the club, she started yelling at my back, "How about a hundred? Just one hundred if you pay now!"

The name Can Can Room conjures up an image of can-can dancers onstage, in ruffled petticoats, kicking their stockinged legs over the heads of the orchestra in the pit below, Toulouse Lautrec smoking French cigarettes in the far corner under a crystal chandelier. The Can Can Room, ooh-la-la!

So when I finally got inside the place, I couldn't help but laugh. It's a little room with cheap fixtures and floor-to-ceiling mirrors on one wall to make it look bigger. Behind the stage is a tacky plywood star on the wall with a number of burned-out light bulbs. The room was almost empty. A few dancers were sitting around with a couple of guys along the back wall; I wasn't even sure they were customers. This was on a warm summer Saturday night when the other Vegas strip clubs would be jumping. In fact, I had just left Badda Bing, which was packed to the rafters.

The only other person in the room was the dancer on stage, who, to my surprise, was really cute. She was topless but wearing a thong, and she appeared to be about 18 or 19. I sat up front and started putting dollars on the stage, since she was basically dancing for me.

The Negotiations Begin

A cocktail waitress approached and told me she could get me a half-hour with any dancer for only $150, because she would take off her "commission." I didn't mention to her that I had already been offered a price of $100 by the lady at the front counter.

Over the next half-hour or so, I watched five dancers in all, of whom only one danced completely nude, despite the fact that I was tipping and this was supposedly a nude club. None of them could dance very well and most of them ignored me, but they were cute young girls, so—in the interest of research for this book, you understand—I started seriously considering those bedroom options.

The more I thought about the deals on offer, the more I felt I had to find out just what this bedroom experience would be. Half-an-hour for $100? In most of the Vegas strip clubs, $100 gets you three songs (about nine minutes) and that's just for lap dancing in a less-than-private VIP booth. This was a naked girl in a bed! Was this the best VIP deal in town? Didn't I, as your dedicated strip-club reporter, owe it to you, my faithful readers, to find out?

So I picked a dancer and told her to tell the cashier that I was prepared to pay $100 for a half-hour. The dancer left and a different waitress showed up to give me a tour of the theme rooms. One was called the "Egyptian Room." It had a big bed, but it was so dark, I immediately discarded it as a choice; I was hoping the other rooms would have at least enough light for me to see the girl I'd chosen. Next up was the "Chinese Room." The lighting was better and again, the big bed was there as promised, but I didn't notice anything particularly Chinese about it. Maybe this was the room preferred by Chinese customers for some reason. Then came the "Jungle Room." One entire wall was covered in leaves—not wallpaper with a leaf design, but actual leaves. I didn't need to see any more rooms. I knew the "Jungle Room" was for me.

As luck would have it, the curtain to the Jungle Room wouldn't close. The curtain rod was broken and had been rigged back up with duct tape or something. So it was back to the Chinese Room!

No sooner had I gone in with the dancer and closed the curtain behind us than another woman entered the room—not the cashier or the first or second waitress, but one I hadn't seen before. She told me that I could pay her the $100 I'd agreed to. I looked at the dancer to see if this was okay with her, as normally in a strip club, you pay the dancer and she tips out the other employees later. But the dancer seemed to have no objections, so I forked over a hundred bucks and the woman exited.

But I'd barely put away my wallet when yet another woman entered the room, saying she had come to "negotiate."

Negotiate? Negotiate what? I told her I'd already paid the hundred bucks I'd agreed to. She informed me that the $100 was just for the room. The dancer wouldn't get any of that money. Now it was time to negotiate for what the dancer would get. She said that if I wanted lap dancing on one of the small chairs in the room, that would be $200 more, and if I wanted a bed dance, $400.

At this point, I realized that I wouldn't find any special bargains for the book and I was getting weary of dealing with the negotiating team. I told her I wasn't interested and she left the room. When I turned to

the dancer to apologize for taking up her time, she told me I could get the bed dance for only $200 and if I didn't have the cash, there was an ATM machine right outside the room.

Then yet another woman entered the room! She and the dancer started a conversation about what a great deal she was offering me, only $200 for a bed dance. Why, that was half-price! I had a feeling she'd been standing outside the door listening to see if the dancer needed help in getting more money out of me. At this point, I just wanted to get out of the joint.

I took $20 out of my wallet, tossed it to the dancer for her trouble, told her I didn't want the half-hour, and left the premises. It had cost me $120 to be in that private bedroom with the dancer of my choice, but I didn't even get a lap dance out of it. My publisher was happy, though. I got the story.

So, sorry, I can't tell you how good a bed dance might be. I can tell you, however, that if you're brave enough to enter into this weird realm of negotiators, the price will keep coming down if you can hold out long enough. I'm just not sure if whatever you ultimately get will be worth whatever you actually pay for it.

This club has been here for decades and I always wondered how it managed to survive, since I've never seen many cars in their parking lot, even on the weekends. Now I know. They've got their own system of making money, with a half-dozen cute young girls, a few private rooms with big comfy beds, and a bunch of ballpoint pens to sweeten the deal.

DÉJÀ VU SHOWGIRLS
3247 Industrial Road, Las Vegas (#23 on map, pg. 39)

Phone: (702) 894-4167
Hours: Mon.–Sat.11 a.m.–6 a.m., Sun. 6 p.m.–4 a.m.
Minimum Age: 18
Valet Parking: Yes; not the best neighborhood, public lot well-lit and trafficked
Cover Charge: $10 before 7 p.m.; locals, $10 bar tab after 7 p.m., non-locals $20 + $10 bar tab
Full Bar: No alcohol served, soft drinks only
Food: Yes
Lap Dances: Main room, $30, 4 songs/$100; Private room, half-hour/$300, full hour/$600, includes non-alcoholic champagne
Website: dejavu.com

Grade of Club: A
Grade of Dancer: Mostly fine, some very fine, some average
SPW: 90%

Snyder Says: Beautiful dancers, incredible pole work, and oil wrestling!

Reviewing the Nude Clubs

Oil-Wrestling Night!

When you go into this place on a Sunday night, you can't help but notice there's an empty plastic blow-up children's swimming pool, not on the stage, but out in the center of the main floor. This is not a small pool. It's like four feet by eight feet, and a good two feet deep. Assuming you're here because you've heard that Sunday is oil-wrestling night, you might deduce that this pool is big enough for … well, for a couple of naked girls to have a wrestling match in.

You've got a long wait. This show doesn't start until sometime after 1 a.m. But when the DJ starts announcing the time has come for the oil wrestling, you want to get a seat as close to that pool as you can. If you're a real brave soul, get a seat at one end of the pool or the other, and you might get picked by one of the girls to oil her up. But don't do this if you're not prepared to become an intimate part of the show. And I'm using "intimate" here in every sense of the word.

Here's what happens. A couple pitchers of water get emptied into the pool. Just clear water, probably warm. That amount of water doesn't even fill the pool to an inch deep. The referee—a dancer in a skimpy little striped referee outfit—comes out and stands beside the pool. Then two girls come out wrapped in towels; when they get poolside, they drop the towels. They're naked. At this point the DJ/announcer is saying the girls' names or something, but who's paying attention to *him*? Each girl picks a lucky guy from the crowd around the pool to oil her up from a small tube of some kind of goop—KY Jelly?

The tension mounts.

The DJ/announcer tells the guys with the "oil" to start dripping that goop on the wrestlers, and smear it all over them, get 'em good and greased up. The way he puts it: "Oil 'em up good, guys, inside and out!"

This is where the show gets interesting. The guys with the goop when I was there were a couple of young nerds, kind of dorky-looking, and they were staring at these stunningly beautiful naked girls in front of them in a state of mild shock. They weren't sure exactly what they were supposed to do, but they tipped that tube of goop over and started dripping it onto their respective girls' titties. Good place to start. The dancers were now instructing them, "Rub it in. Smear it around." And the guys were still not quite sure they understood. Were they actually supposed to touch them?

You betcha, and they definitely got into it. They started rubbing that slippery goop all over these gorgeous girls' bodies—up, down, front, back, all over.

Then the ref tells the girls to get in the pool and assume the starting position, which is down on all fours, facing each other and ready to rumble. The guys with the goop were still staring at their girls in disbelief. (Did I really just have my hands all over that girl? Have I died and gone to heaven? How did I get this job?)

The ref says go, the girls go at it, and they're really rasslin', seriously trying to get each other pinned, both squirming and squealing like … well, like a couple of greased-up naked girls wrestling in a wading pool!

Now wrestling is not exactly a graceful art form, but when the wrestlers are a couple of angels with athletes' bodies, naked and shaved smooth all over, there is absolutely no position, none, that even begins to look the least bit awkward or unattractive. In fact, if you weren't sitting there with your mouth agape that this scene is actually happening before your eyes, you'd want to shout a hundred times during the first round alone, "Wait! Could you hold that pose for a moment?"

We haven't even gotten to round two yet, but let me just say that without qualification, this is the most outrageous show in Vegas today. Not for the faint of heart.

Déjà Vu is an international chain of clubs in more than 80 locations. (Little Darlings, also located in Las Vegas, is one of its sister clubs.) I've been in dozens of Déjà Vu clubs in the U.S. and most are modeled on the same format. It's a hugely successful chain.

Because there's real money behind Déjà Vu, it's a bit classier than most of the nude clubs in Vegas. The facilities are clean, roomy, comfortable, and well-maintained. The main stage is big enough for the girls to truly dance, with lots of seats on the rail. The lighting on the main stage is also better than in most strip clubs today, where dark is the norm. With the lap dancing taking place off the main floor, the club seems to realize that the stage show is the big attraction.

Two smaller stages with poles get used when the club is crowded, meaning Friday and Saturday nights only. Dancers on these stages do three-song sets, instead of the standard two songs, on the main stage. These are great stages for watching dancers close-up. In only three nude clubs in Las Vegas can you see three-song sets and this is one of them. The other two are Little Darlings and Talk of the Town.

Perhaps you don't know how important a three-song set is. For topless dancing, two-song sets are fine, but for a nude strip show, three-song sets are far superior for maximizing the erotic punch. In the first song, the dancer just teases, flashing her tits and finally getting topless at the end. In the second song, she dances topless, but spends most of her time taking her panties off, teasing the boys by pulling them down, then back up again, with lots of sexy posing. Then she removes her panties and dances the third song completely naked.

If you're not into watching strippers, this probably sounds gratuitous to you—but it should be gratuitous. There's no practical reason why it should take a dancer three minutes to remove her panties, but this is what striptease is all about. I only wish the main-stage dancers would do three-song sets.

Pole dancing is primo on the weekends at Déjà Vu

Because no alcohol is served, dancers can be 18 and work here and the crowd is generally younger than you find in the drinking establishments. Many of these girls will be working in the topless clubs as soon as they turn 21, simply because they can make a lot more money hustling middle-aged guys with fat wallets who want to drink.

When it comes to factors like beauty and dancing talent, however, Déjà Vu is one of the premier nude clubs in Las Vegas. All of these girls are cute as hell, with gorgeous athletic bodies and not an ounce of fat on any of them, and they can all dance. They exhibit more personality, energy, and even humor than you generally find in the more jaded dancers in the topless clubs.

Does Déjà Vu have some sort of school for dancers? The pole work is incredible and the floor work is dynamite. Every one of these girls has the moves down.

The silicone factor is also pretty low. If you're looking for big tits, hit the topless bars. You'll see a few stacked girls here, some enhanced, but even the big tits are mostly natural, while the majority of the Déjà Vu girls still have their cute little natural titties, a big plus in my opinion. It's sad to think that some of them will be getting boob jobs a few years from now so they can compete with all the tit queens in the high-end jiggle joints.

The hustle factor is also lower. These girls are used to having lots of young guys in the crowd, many of whom don't have $30 to spring for a couch dance. So they solicit the older guys, especially any who show up in sports jackets, but they're not pushy or persistent.

A smaller stage in the back of the club is used when it's crowded or for bachelor parties. The victim—the dude who's either getting married or graduating or whatever—gets tied bare-chested to a chair on the stage while a half-dozen dancers take turns squirming all over him as his buddies cheer them on.

Lap dances are either couch or "bed dances," priced at $30 per song, and take place in the "theme rooms" away from the main floor. These rooms are not only themeless, they're not even rooms—just small cubicles with open entries, furnished with either a couch or a "bed," actually more of a small Naugahyde-covered futon with a wedge-shaped cushion on it. One room had a framed print of a desert scene, something you might find at Target for $19.95. I asked a dancer what the room's theme was and she said, "I guess this is our Southwestern room."

The overall feeling of the place is fun and friendly and high on the erotic scale. These dancers not only seem to love turning guys on, but to have a good time doing it. Déjà Vu has recently begun hosting an amateur contest on Wednesdays at midnight.

A limited menu of food items is available—pizza, chicken wings, egg rolls, and the like, all priced at five or six bucks. In addition to the free soft drinks, you can purchase juices, energy drinks, and non-alcoholic beer for four bucks.

Déjà Vu's Erotic Heritage Museum

Right next door to Déjà Vu, you'll find the Erotic Heritage Museum. This place opened in August 2008 and displays the erotic art collection of Harry Mohney, who founded the Déjà Vu chain, and Ted McIlvenna, an international collector of erotica. This is a serious museum and if you have any interest in erotic art or its history, you should visit.

The general-admission charge is $20, or $15 for seniors, students, and Las Vegas residents. You can become a member for an annual fee ($100, or $50 for students or seniors), which allows you free admission any time. (Right now, you can also purchase a ticket for the museum for only $5 at Déjà Vu or Little Darlings.)

According to the director of the museum, between them, Mohney and McIlvenna have 30 warehouses filled with erotica, so the exhibits change regularly. The current display includes everything from fine-art drawings, paintings, photographs, and sculpture to pin-up art, old movie posters, books, periodicals, sex toys, costumes, fetish equipment, and even life-size mannequins wearing or using some of the outfits and devices. There's also a wall of newspaper clippings that report on famous obscenity busts and trials.

Las Vegas is known for its weird museums. The Elvis Museum,

unfortunately, is gone, as is Debbie Reynolds Hollywood Movie Museum and that great casino gambling museum that used to be at the Tropicana. But we're still the only town with an Atomic Testing Museum and a Liberace Museum, and now we have a kinky sex museum to boot. If you live in Las Vegas, you should seriously consider becoming a member. This place deserves our support.

DIAMOND CABARET
3177 S. Highland Dr., Las Vegas (#24 on map, pg. 39)

Phone: (702) 731-2365
Hours: 6 p.m.–6 a.m.
Minimum Age: 18
Valet Parking: No; dark lot next door to club, attendant out front
Cover Charge: $20; locals, $10; both prices include soft drinks
Full Bar: No alcohol served, soft drinks only
Food: No
Lap Dances: VIP room, half-hour/$300, 45 min/$400, full hour/ $500
Website: None

Grade of Club: D
Grade of Dancer: Mostly fine, some average
SPW: 50%

Snyder Says: A relaxed VIP-room club with
a nice selection of dancers.

Reviewing the Nude Clubs

It's midnight on a Saturday and your wife went to bed early. Nothing's on TV. The idea of going to a strip club appeals to you, but you really don't feel like putting up with the Saturday-night crowds, noise, and hustle. What you'd really like is just a relaxing hour in a VIP room with a sexy girl who will leave you with some fantasies to take home.

Isn't there some smaller quieter club you could go to with good-looking dancers, where you could go in, take your pick, have your fun, and go home?

Consider the Diamond Cabaret.

This is a very small club. It was renovated at some point in the past couple of years. Most of the remodel of the main room consisted of painting the non-mirrored surfaces black, adding a DJ booth, and putting in more comfortable chairs. Cabs are always parked out front whenever I drive by, and I have a feeling that most of the business are tourists brought in by taxi. This isn't a locals place. Even on weekend nights, it's not crowded.

Essentially, this is a club for guys who want a private VIP-room experience. The rooms are small, but comfortable and secluded. Each cubicle has a diaphanous curtain at the entry, which you can close, and a couch. Since there are so few customers in the place and no bouncer is standing there watching you, the VIP rooms are very private if that's what you're looking for.

A dancer is always on stage, but if seven or eight women are in the club, only three or four actually perform on stage—the others do VIP-room shows only. So if you're primarily going to watch the stage show, all the dancers will cycle through within 20 to 30 minutes. Unless you want to watch the same dancers again and again, you won't get much of a show.

None of the dancers exhibit much talent, but they have the basic stripper moves down and most are pretty cute. There's a friendly feeling to this place and you won't be hustled non-stop. If you like VIP rooms and that's all you're looking for, you might want to check this place out.

LITTLE DARLINGS
1514 Western Ave., Las Vegas (#25 on map, pg. 39)

Phone: (702) 366-1141
Hours: Mon.–Sat. 11 a.m.–6 a.m., Sun. 6 p.m.–4 a.m.
Minimum Age: 18
Valet Parking: Yes; seedy neighborhood, well-lit, high-traffic area
Cover Charge: $30; locals, $10; both prices include soft drinks
Full Bar: No alcohol served, soft drinks only
Food: Yes
Lap Dances: Main room, $20; VIP room, 3 songs/$100, half-hour/
$300, full hour/$500
Website: littledarlingsnv.com

Grade of Club: A
Grade of Dancer: Mostly fine, some very fine, some average
SPW: 90%

Snyder Says: Hot stage show, dollar dances,
and "cooterball."

Reviewing the Nude Clubs

Little Darlings is part of the Déjà Vu chain and it's one of my favorite nude clubs in Las Vegas. The main stage show is great. The dancers are young, beautiful, and talented. The disc jockey is funny. And the club always feels like a party, thanks to the games, contests, and promotions they run.

Cooterball

Take "cooterball." I was standing up to leave one night when the DJ announced the cooterball contest. Three dancers wearing nothing but their platform heels came out onto the stage, each carrying an empty plastic cup, the same small cup the waitresses here use to serve soft drinks. I sat back down.

Two of the dancers sat down on the stage, one in front of each side pole, spread their legs, and set their little plastic cups on the stage in front of their … well, their cooters. The third dancer climbed about six feet up the center pole and placed her cup, more or less, in front of her cooter, though it wasn't easy to see her cup, what with her up in the air like that and straddling the pole the way strippers do.

The DJ explained the rules of cooterball. Any guy who could throw a crumpled dollar bill into one of the cups would win a prize. The prize for getting a dollar into an easy cup on the stage would be a Little Darlings T-shirt. But the prize for getting a dollar into the cup of the dancer up the pole, who was now spinning at a pretty good clip, would be a Little Darlings VIP membership card, entitling the winner to unlimited free admission, including free drinks, for three months.

As the dollar bills started flying, I calculated the value of these gambles. (What can I say? Too many years as a professional gambler.) I figured that the T-shirt might cost about $9, so risking $1 to win it, I'd be getting odds of 8-to-1 (since you don't get back the dollar you risk in your attempt to win the shirt). Now I'm really good at flinging balls of paper into little cups, as it's a skill I've practiced at home. Professional gamblers often develop unusual skills in order to win prop bets with other gamblers, and this just happens to be one of my talents. The problem was I didn't want a T-shirt. I'd never wear it, so the prize had no real value to me. If the payout was $9 cash, instead of a $9 shirt, I would have quickly tossed a crumpled bill into each of those cups in front of the sitting girls' cooters and collected both prizes. The competition was rank amateur at best, with the stage quickly becoming littered with crumpled bills and most of the shots—even from the guys perfectly positioned to hit the target—not even close.

As for getting a dollar bill into the cup of the dancer spinning on the pole, you could only catch an occasional glimpse of the cup, and on top of the timing difficulty was the distraction factor. That naked dancer spinning on the pole was absolutely gorgeous—perfect breasts, an ass as fine as can be, long beautiful legs … They could run this contest for a year without anyone managing to dunk a buck into that barely visible spinning plastic cup.

Still, I calculated that the return on a $1 investment would be worth about $900, based on 90 days free admission to the club at $10 a pop—the locals' admission fee. Of course, that was assuming I'd come every day. If I adjusted the potential value for the number of days I'd more likely show up, then further adjusted for the difficulty and distraction factors—I mean this girl was so damn hot—I estimated that the actual value of this $1 bet was not $900, but about $1.72.

The DJ announced that the contest was about to end. There must have been a hundred crumpled bills on the stage, and both of the stationary cups had already been hit. Since the potential reward far outweighed the risk, I crumpled a dollar bill and launched it toward the target.

Bingo!

The guy sitting next to me, who'd already wasted some $20 attempting to win that VIP membership card, said, "How the fuck did you do that?"

Winning the VIP card kind of blew my angle on the cooterball story, which I was planning to expose as no more than a variation on the old carnie quarter-toss scam. I was going to say don't waste your money trying to win that VIP membership. Now, I'm just waiting for cooterball to become an Olympic event.

The main stage here is a big three-pole affair where you'll see some of the sexiest dancing in town. The pole work, especially, will take your breath away, because so many of the dancers here are superb athletes. Many of the dancers are under 21 and the silicone factor is minimal. This club—like Déjà Vu—will primarily appeal to guys who like watching real dancers.

The club is modern, well-lit, and comfortable, and there's rarely much lag time between dancers. On a typical set, a dancer starts out in a skimpy outfit and gets topless not long into the first song. She performs most of the second song nude. Most dancers do a lot of floor work on the second song, concentrating their teasing on the guys on the rail and tipping. A dollar tip goes a long way here.

If you're into watching *striptease*, as opposed to just naked girls, you'll really love this place on the weekends. On the mini-stage in the back of the room, used only on Friday and Saturday nights (or on other nights when sufficiently crowded), dancers do three-song sets, instead of the more typical two songs. With no backstage area—since the mini-stage is just a small platform out in the audience—you actually get to see the dancers removing their outfits. Instead of just watching them walk off stage between songs and come back naked, you get to watch their panties come off. If you're going to have nude dancing, this is the way to do it. Dancers should make the boys beg for the pussy, ache for it, pay for it! (See my comments in the Déjà Vu Show-girls review regarding three-song sets.)

This stage is also great for guys who like to sit on the rail and watch dancers close up. The stage is small enough that the dancer is automatically close to every guy sitting on the rail, and because there are fewer rail seats, tippers get more attention than from dancers on the main stage. You won't see the same high-energy acrobatic dancing on this stage that you'll see on the main stage, but the floor work is as close up as it gets.

The Tuesday Night Amateur Contest

Tuesday night at Little Darlings features the Amateur Strip Contest, which generally starts around 12:30 a.m. Technically, this is an audition night for dancers trying to get a job at the club. Amateur nights at strip clubs are just about always audition nights and in most cases, the "amateurs" are actually professional dancers from other clubs who already have the outfits and know all the moves. Not so at Little Darlings. This is an entry-level club for young women attempting to start careers as strippers, so few of the dancers you'll see in the contest are pros. As they don't have the stripper moves down and they're not adept at the poles at all, there's a fun factor to watching real amateurs compete that's absent when you watch pros. And they are definitely auditioning for jobs. I saw the winner one Tuesday night dancing in the regular line-up on Wednesday night.

For about a year, this contest was called the Naughty Schoolgirl Contest, and in keeping with the theme, all the regular dancers, and even the cocktail waitresses, wore plaid micro-minis. I was in Catholic schoolboy heaven all night long! Sad to say they recently abandoned the schoolgirl theme, but the contest is still fun, basically the same thing without the plaid skirts. Because these are amateurs, the DJ/MC mercifully gives each contestant only about 30 seconds to get out of her skimpy duds and dance. Also, because these are amateurs, some of the contestants get naked and some don't. One night, with six dancers competing, two of the six didn't get naked. One took her top off briefly, but the other never removed her top or bottom. It didn't surprise me, though, when both ended up among the three money winners, because they were the two cutest girls on the stage and could dance better than the others. The winners are decided by audience applause and the crowd knew talent when they saw it.

Your Dollar Goes a Long Way Here

Little Darlings is a great club for any guy on a budget. If you're a local, the entry fee is just $10 (and only $5 on Tuesday nights. It's $25 if you're not a local (and they will check your ID at the door), but that also covers unlimited soft drinks. It'll take a couple of hours to sit through the stage sets of all the dancers, and even if you sit up front and tip a buck to each, it'll only run you $15 to $20 more.

Lap dances here are only $20 (as opposed to $30 at Déjà Vu) and once an hour or so, the DJ announces 2-for-1 lap-dance specials, or sometimes 2 for $30. Lap dancing takes place in semi-private booths in back. One of the VIP rooms has a neon sign over the entrance: "Roman Orgy." This room is for guys who pay $100 or more, but the cubicles in the Roman Orgy room aren't much different from those in the regular VIP area. Each cubicle in the Roman Orgy room has a comfortable couch and a diaphanous curtain across the entry. You can expect higher mileage dances at the $100+ rates.

In addition to frequent 2-for-1 lap dances, the DJ also announces an occasional "dollar dance time," where all the dancers come out onto the main floor and do full-contact lap dances for a buck each, with each dance lasting about 30 seconds. When the DJ says "switch," it's time for the dancers to move from one guy to the next. This goes on for five minutes or so, and all the dancers stay in action the whole time, with many guys getting a half-dozen or more dollar lap dances, all from different girls. Some girls aren't wearing their g-strings, but even those who are usually pull them down, or flash their pussies while they dance. It's so much fun to sit there with a fistful of dollars, in this smorgasbord of flesh, just to see which Little Darling shows up in your lap next.

Rock Naked?

The club has recently been advertising Wednesday nights as "Rock Naked" night, where you can meet the hottest local rock bands "before they get famous." I was really excited about the prospect of seeing modern strippers dancing to live rock music, as Vegas has a really active rock scene with quite a few great local bands. Prior to the 1960s, strippers typically danced to live music provided by local jazz combos, with the drummers rimshotting the bumps and grinds. The closest thing we've seen to it in Vegas was the now-gone Forty Deuce scene at Mandalay Bay. So, I was revved up on the idea of seeing the Little Darlings dancers—some of the best in the business—playing off the licks of our local rockers.

What a disappointment. No live band was playing when I went there on a recent Wednesday night, so I asked one of the floor managers when the band would show up.

"The bands are here," he said. He pointed to a couple of long tables that had been set up against one wall, where half a dozen guys were sitting, watching the show. Each table had a placard on it with a band's name.

"When do they play?" I asked.

"They're not going to play," he said.

"What are they here for?"

"Just meet and greet," he said. "You can go over and say hello to them. They're like the honored guests tonight."

Why? These guys aren't Aerosmith, or even Alien Ant Farm. These are just local dudes sitting there in their jeans and T-shirts, drinking Pepsi Colas like everyone else in the audience, and no one seemed much interested in meeting and greeting them. I think they were even wondering what the hell they were doing here. I'm not listing Wednesday night at this club as a special event, because personally, I don't get it.

But this club is run by some of the smartest operators in the business. They know that their customer base includes a lot of guys under

21 who aren't sitting there with wallets full of $20s and $100s, and they know how to get whatever money there is to extract. This place works well for both its dancers and customers. The club recently added a food menu that includes $2 burgers, $7 BBQ dinners, and $7 full breakfasts. I haven't tried the food here yet, so I can't comment on the quality.

I have to give Little Darlings my vote as one of the best all-around strip clubs in Las Vegas, from just about every perspective. The main stage show is second to none. The mini-stage show is dynamite. Their dancers are as good-looking and talented as you'll find anywhere. The fun factor is high and you can't beat the prices. If you can live without booze and you're not hooked on the high-mileage lap dances you get in the topless clubs, this is one of the clubs that should be at the top of your list when you're in the mood for getting turned on.

PALOMINO CLUB
1848 Las Vegas Blvd. N., North Las Vegas (#26 on map, pg. 39)

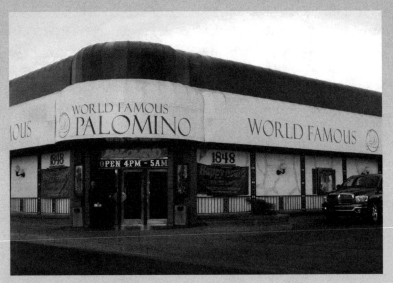

Phone: (702) 642-2984
Hours: 4 p.m.–5 a.m.
Minimum Age: 21
Valet Parking: Yes; dicey neighborhood, well-lit and across from casino on busy street
Cover Charge: Sun.–Thurs. locals free, $10 after 9 p.m. Fri. and Sat.; non-locals free before 9 p.m., $20 after
Full Bar: Yes
Food: No
Lap Dances: Main room, $20/topless; VIP room, 3 songs/$100, half-hour/$225, full hour/$450
Website: palominolv.com

Grade of Club: A
Grade of Dancer: Mostly fine, some very fine, some average, some below average
SPW: 80%

Snyder Says: Most improved club in Vegas.
Hot dancers. Excellent stage show. And booze!

Reviewing the Nude Clubs

Twenty-five years ago before I lived in this town, I used to come to this club whenever I visited Las Vegas. Vegas was a much smaller town then—no megaresorts, no family vacationers—and the Palomino was a classic strip joint. The dancers were top-of-the-line strippers—beautiful professionals with great bodies. They had no customer contact and didn't hustle drinks or VIP-room shows. Instead of lap dances, the Palomino dancers did full strip routines, starting from gowns and gloves and getting down to peeling off their stockings—the whole bit. They took their time, teased and pleased, and knew how to work the crowd. And it all came off.

Today, the Palomino is the only strip club in Las Vegas that allows both alcoholic beverages and nude dancing. As Las Vegas' oldest strip club, opened in 1969, the nude-dancing license and full bar were grandfathered in when the law changed.

At some point through the years, this club went downhill, way downhill, and I quit going. In fact, if it wasn't for this book, I never would have returned. But this club has new owners since my last visit and the change has been dramatic. The Palomino may be Las Vegas' single most improved strip club in the past five years.

The décor is more high-tech than it used to be—darker with more flashing lights—but the overall lighting is bright enough that the stage dancers are well-lit on a big stage with lots of rail seats. The look is halfway between the '70s disco ambience of the typical high-tech gentlemen's clubs and the warmer, more comfortable, nude clubs like Déjà Vu, where the overall feeling is more like a showroom than a rave.

All the stage dancers I saw in the couple hours I was there were hot. A few of the women who didn't perform onstage were below average, but they were strictly working the crowd for lap dances.

Because this club serves booze, customers must be 21 or older. But the dancers only have to be 18! That age allowance was grandfathered in with the nude dancing and drinking allowance. With a drinking crowd, the feel of the place is more like a topless club. Lap dances take place out on the main floor and cost $20, but are done topless, not nude. Dances in the VIP room are nude. The VIP room isn't private, just a typical dark room with multiple comfortable semi-private booths.

Reviewing the Nude Clubs

If you want to drink alcohol and watch nude dancers, this is the one place in Vegas you can do so, and I highly recommend it. My compliments to the new owners and managers for turning this place around.

Urban Nite

A secret society of men in this world like big women. If you happen to be among them, especially if you happen to like big black women, then Urban Nite at the Palomino is the only strip club show that will ever satisfy you. This show happens upstairs in the club's Penthouse. The room opens at 10 p.m., but don't expect the show to start any time before 11. On weekends, this room features an all-male review, the Palomino Stallions. But on Wednesday and Thursday nights, one of the male dancers, who goes by the name Foreplay, hosts a bevy of big-booty black dancers, who put on one of the wildest, full-nude, in-your-face (and I mean that literally!) strip shows I've ever seen anywhere.

In order to enter the Palomino Penthouse, there's a separate $20 admission fee, which buys you a bracelet that gets you past the door-man/bouncer. *Note: Once you have that bracelet on, you will only be allowed into the Penthouse, not into the Palomino's regular strip club area downstairs.* You cannot come and go between the two rooms, even on nights when the regular strip club has no admission fee. If you want to go from the Penthouse to the downstairs club, they will take the bracelet away from you and you must pay $20 again to go back to the Penthouse. In my opinion … dumb policy.

I can't really write about some of the off-the-chart antics of the dancers—this is a *family* strip-club guide, after all—so suffice it to say that Urban Nite is wild fun and even if you're not into BBWs, you'll likely have a good time just watching the crazy scene. The Penthouse has its own full bar with the same drink pricing as downstairs (domestic beer $5.50), plus its own private VIP room and its own DJ, spinning rap and hip-hop all night long. And Foreplay, who MCs the show, is funny as hell.

I stayed for about an hour and a half of the show and as I was exiting, the Penthouse doorman asked me why I was leaving so early. I told him it was late and I was going home. He said, "Don't leave now, man. You ain't seen nothing yet. This show really gets wild as the night wears on!"

Maybe next time …

The Palomino, an innovator for years, recently instituted Urban Nite.

PUSSYCAT'S
3525 Procyon St., Las Vegas (#27 on map, pg. 39)

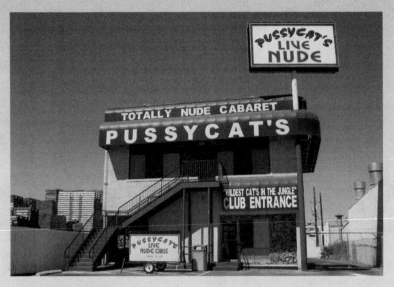

Phone: (702) 365-1408
Hours: noon–6 a.m. daily
Minimum Age: 18
Valet Parking: No; well-lit private fenced lot
Cover Charge: $10
Full Bar: No alcohol served, soft drinks only
Food: No
Lap Dances: $30 (2-for-1); see description for VIP room policy
Website: None

Grade of Club: D
Grade of Dancer: Fine and average
SPW: 25%

Snyder Says: It sort of looks like a strip club ...

Reviewing the Nude Clubs

As soon as you see the sign outside this club that says, "100's of Gorgeous Girls," you know something's not right. The building is about the size of a two-car garage. How do hundreds of dancers fit in there? They'd have to be stacked on top of each other.

It turns out this is another VIP-room club, similar to the Can Can Room, only more up front with customers about the operation. The first clue is the good-looking girl at the door who tells you that she's your "tour guide."

"This is where the girls dance," she says, walking you through a plain front room where a man is standing behind a counter, into a small room where a pretty girl in a thong is wiggling around on a small floor-level stage. Maybe a dozen chairs are strewn around the room and two customers are watching the dancer. My home office is twice the size of this room.

The tour continues. "This is the lap-dance room"—smaller and darker, furnished with a few easy chairs, and no customers or dancers.

"This is one of our VIP rooms. It's very private." She walks into this room and invites me to sit on the couch with her. I do. "If you get this room, you'll be alone with the dancer you choose and you have to talk with her about exactly what you want."

I asked her if she could give me some idea of what the prices might be for this room. She told me I'd have to talk with the manager about the VIP-room prices and we exited and went back to the lobby.

The manager told me that the VIP room costs $150 for 15 minutes, $275 for 30 minutes, or $375 for an hour. But because I was a local, he could knock $25 off the prices for the half-hour or hour. He also said that those prices covered the room only and I'd have to negotiate with whatever dancer I chose for whatever I wanted her to do in that room. He said that this wasn't really a strip club so much as a VIP-room club, and that they were essentially offering a more private VIP-room experience than the strip clubs.

So what do I make of this joint? I do feel I was dealt with ethically, insofar as there was no attempt to get any money out of me until the whole deal was clearly explained, unlike the Can Can Room, where it took five people and 30 minutes and cost me $130 to get the story.

But is it worth $250 for a half-hour, when that just covers the room and the dancer is extra? This isn't the way a normal VIP room operates. I'm only including this club in my reviews because they do, in fact, have a stage show and you can go in to watch the few dancers who are there, if that's what you want. It looks like a small strip club from the outside. It feels like something else on the inside.

SHERI'S CABARET
(formerly Tally-Ho)
2580 S. Highland Dr., Las Vegas (#28 on map, pg. 39)

Phone: (702) 792-1400
Hours: 3 p.m.–7 a.m. daily
Minimum Age: 18
Valet Parking: No; well-lit private fenced lot with attendant
Cover Charge: $20; locals, $10; both prices include soft drinks
Full Bar: No alcohol served, soft drinks only
Food: No
Lap Dances: Main room, $35, $20/locals; VIP room, 3 songs/$100, half-hour/$225, full hour/$400
Website: sheriscabaret.com

Grade of Club: A
Grade of Dancer: Mostly fine, some average, some very fine, some below average
SPW: 40%

Snyder Says: Heavy on the hustle.

It's a slow night. I sit down and within minutes a babe in lingerie is in my lap, asking me if I want to have some fun in the VIP. She's cute, but I say no thanks, not right now, I want to watch the show awhile. She starts telling me how much better the show could be in the VIP room and the waitress appears. "Would you like to buy a drink for Bambi?" she asks. I say no thanks and the dancer abruptly leaps out of my lap. "I'm outta here!" she says.

Two minutes later, another dancer is in my lap and here comes the waitress again!

Five or six years ago, this club was a dive called the Tally-Ho. It changed ownership, became Sheri's Cabaret, and started undergoing renovations. I visited the club during that phase and I liked it a lot. The funky little room with the small platform stage and the big mismatched but comfy easy chairs was a lot more intimate than the other nude clubs in Vegas and it was definitely wilder. With no backstage area, when a dancer finished her stage set, she hopped right down into the audience naked and jumped into some guy's lap. It was the only place in town with nude lap dances right there on the main floor.

Unfortunately, the renovation was completed in 2006 and now the club looks exactly like all the other high-tech gentlemen's clubs in town. I'm sure the dancers appreciate having a cleaner environment to work in, but as a customer, I actually preferred the old, wilder, under-renovation version.

One thing that hasn't changed is that the dancers in this club are probably the most aggressive in town at hustling lap dances and VIP-room shows. Don't be surprised if a dancer just plops into your lap and starts her sales pitch. If it's a slow night, you'll find one dancer after another in your lap, followed in short order by the cocktail waitress, trying to sell you a drink for the dancer. Since this is a nude club, only soft drinks are served, and though your drinks are free, a Coke for a dancer costs you $10.

Sheri's has a unique policy of charging locals and out-of-towners different rates for lap dances. Locals (they check all IDs at the door) get a wristband, so the girls know to charge you $20 for lap dances. No wristband? The lap dances cost $35.

What I generally like most about the nude clubs are the stage shows; they usually have bigger stages with better lighting and more talented dancers. But the lighting in Sheri's Cabaret is an exception. This club has generally good-looking dancers, but the stage lighting is very dim—mostly blue overhead spots—and the large video screens on either side of the stage that display the music videos are much brighter than the stage lighting. The two strobe-light poles at the rear of the stage are a bigger problem and they really ought to be shit-canned. If you sit close to the stage when those strobes get turned on, they flash right in your eyes, so you have to turn away and stop watching the dancer on stage until they're turned off again. I'm not the only one who never sits on the rail in this club; very few men do. Stage dancers here are not well-tipped. This club's SPW would be much higher if they'd fix the lighting.

The VIP rooms in Sheri's are private—you're alone in a small separate room with the dancer of your choice—but they have glass doors, so they don't actually feel private, especially on a crowded weekend evening when other dancers and customers are walking by in the hallway.

TALK OF THE TOWN
1238 Las Vegas Blvd. S., Las Vegas (#29 on map, pg. 39)

Phone: (702) 385-1800
Hours: 4 p.m.–2 a.m.
Minimum Age: 18
Valet Parking: No; but well-lit lot on busy street
Cover Charge: Before 8 p.m. $7; after 8 p.m. non-locals, $17, locals, $12; all prices includes one soft drink
Full Bar: No alcohol served, soft drinks only
Food: No; some snack items
Lap Dances: Main room, $10; see description for VIP room policy
Website: talkofthetownlv.com

Grade of Club: A
Grade of Dancer: Mostly fine and very fine, some average
SPW: 90%

Snyder Says: This place is starting to live up to its name.

Whatever happened to watching dancers take off their clothes slowly? Having visited every strip club in Las Vegas (and I've been going to strip clubs for 45 years), I can tell you it's a lost art form. So if you haven't been to Talk of the Town for a while, you're in for a pleasant surprise. This club has put the tease back into striptease: It's the only club in Vegas where all dancers do all three-song sets. That's every set, every dancer, every night of the week. (See my comments on three-song sets in my Déjà Vu Showgirls review, pg. 138.)

Three Songs, Hot Lights, and Sweat

On top of that, Talk of the Town has the best stage lighting for watching dancers of any club in Vegas, the only one that illuminates the stage with a white spot—and not a flashing white spot. The gorgeous girls here are all women you want to see well-lit.

These dancers don't have the room on stage to exhibit the kind of acrobatic dancing and fancy pole work you see on the bigger stages, but that scorching panty play during the three-song set more than makes up for any drawbacks of space. All the dancers at Talk of the Town are playful and creative, and under that hot white spotlight, you can actually see them glistening by the end of their sets, and sweat is just so sexy in itself.

Another pleasant surprise for those who haven't been here in a while is that lap dances are only $10. And these aren't the quickie lap dances the club used to offer for $5, but full-song, topless, full-contact lap dances for ten bucks! (Nude for $20.)

It's the regular price all night every night. And did I mention that these dancers are as fine as you'll find anywhere?

Talk of the Town is a small club and no one comes here for the plush decor. The wooden stage is about eight by eight feet, with a stripper pole in the center and a brass rail around the perimeter. The ceiling is unfinished, with exposed air ducts and rafters. All the walls are painted flat black, with large framed mirrors hanging everywhere. There's a life-size white-plaster statue of Aphrodite on which someone has painted black eyebrows. There are 20 small marble-top cocktail tables and comfortable lap dance chairs. All in all, this place looks like a beatnik coffee house, reminiscent of the joints I used to give poetry readings in when I lived in San Francisco. It's a pleasant change from the disco throb of the typical high-tech gentlemen's clubs.

Talk of the Town has four VIP rooms, all private. Two have humungous bean-bag beds that literally take up the whole room. One has a swiveling lounge chair. Another is set up for private shower shows.

If you see something you like at Talk of the Town, lap dances are only $10.

A dancer quoted a VIP room price of $199 for a half-hour and $398 for an hour, but told me different dancers could quote different prices. Because everything about this club is so unusual—the $17 cover charge, the absence of any attempt at mimicking the look of the other Vegas strip joints, the three-song sets, the white spotlight on the stage dancers, the $10 lap dances on the main floor, and now the $199 charge for one of the atypical VIP rooms, with the actual charge being at the discretion of the dancer, not set by the club—I decided to test the VIP room just to make sure there wouldn't be any unpleasant price-hike surprises.

I'm happy to report that all the surprises in the VIP room at Talk of the Town were more than pleasant. This is a really fun and friendly club with a great stage show and the best-priced lap dances in town, and I'll definitely go back.

Part Two

Topless Pools

9

Overview of the Pools

It's a fact of life that in this country, female nipples are big entertainment. In Europe, no big deal. In America, big BIG deal. Now, I'm all for the idealistic notion that topless pools are about giving women the same freedom to bare their chests to the glorious sunshine that men have always enjoyed. But let's face it, that's not what topless pools are about to American guys. Topless pools are about us guys getting to look at girls' titties. If we're to pay the outrageous admission fees the topless pools charge, compared to the fees (if any) of the casinos' regular pools, believe me, we're going for the tit show.

Why else would men be charged $20 for admission to Flamingo's GO Pool or Stratosphere's Beach Club 25, while ladies are admitted free? Why are ladies admitted for $10 to Rio's Sapphire pool and Mandalay Bay's Moorea Beach Club, while men have to pay $50? Fifty bucks! Just to go for a dip? I'll tell you why these price inequities exist—because guys will pay a lot more to see nipples than women will pay to get sunshine on them. Women could care less about seeing other women's tits. The casinos catering to the American crowd let women into the topless pool areas for a song, hoping they'll provide the show we dudes are paying top dollar for.

American-Style vs. European-Style

So first off, in order to compare apples to apples, I categorize the topless pools in Vegas as either "European-style" or "American-style." Any pool I categorize as European-style probably won't appeal to readers of this guide. At a European-style topless pool, there'll be too many nipples you'd rather not see, let alone pay to see. I work from the assumption that you're a guy who wants to get his money's worth.

You go to a European-style pool to relax. You go to an American-style pool to party. At a European-style pool, the ambience is more serene than saturnalian. The music is subdued. Bathers lounge around the edges of the pool where the water barely shows a ripple. People catch up on their summer reading and even snooze in the deck lounges. At an American-style pool, on the other hand, the air-rattling sound system is cranked up to encourage dancing, with a DJ spinning top hits. Lots of beach balls are provided to discourage bathers from lounging, beer is sold by the bucket, and cocktail servers in teeny bikinis

Stratosphere
Beach Club 25

" ... all of these pool features are secondary. Far more important in rating a topless pool is the industry-standard ANEI (or the Adjusted Nipple Entertainment Index) "

make the rounds with shots and shooters.

I compare the entry fees and describe the pools and sunbathing areas, the drink and food options and prices, and anything else the various pools might provide. I don't list all the prices for cabana rentals or day beds, which often change, depending on the day of week, expected crowd conditions, and whether you rent for a full or half-day. I provide phone numbers for the topless pools that you can call to inquire about cabana and day bed rentals and to make reservations. But all of these pool features are secondary. Far more important in rating a topless pool is the industry-standard ANEI (or the Adjusted Nipple Entertainment Index).

Counting Nipples

Male nipples don't figure into the nipple count. Let's face it, men's nipples have no entertainment value. They don't do any of the multitude of wonderfully amusing things that women's nipples do, which I'm sure I don't have to enumerate.

When counting female nipples in a pool environment, statisticians have determined that the Raw Nipple Count (RNC), in and of itself, is a very poor gauge of entertainment value. I discovered the truth of this on my first visit to a European-style topless pool, where the only female nipples on display were on the chest of an overweight fiftyish lady sunning herself in a deck chair with a cocktail in one hand and a cigarette in a rhinestone-studded cigarette holder in the other. She had a beautiful golden tan, but with her ample belly, her 50-year-old tits might best be described as fried eggs on a barrel. Not nipples I'd pay to see.

So, instead of using the RNC, or the Raw Nipple Count, I use what we in the industry call the SGNC, or the Stripper-Grade Nipple Count. If the female owner of the nipples I encounter at a topless pool would not, could not, or should not (in my opinion) be dancing in a strip club, then her nipples are assumed to have the same entertainment value as my nipples—which is zip—and they don't figure into the count.

I must stipulate that any assessment of what constitutes stripper-grade nipples is necessarily subjective. My wife came with me to some of the topless pools I visited and she felt that my standards were rather strict in this regard. I had to agree with her that some of the nipples I discarded from the SGNC could, in fact, be entertaining to some men and that the females in question could probably get work in some of the Vegas strip clubs that hire dancers on the lower end of the body spectrum. But if I'm paying to see nipples, I want top-quality nipples only. So when I say stripper grade, I mean top-of-the-line stripper grade. That's the only way a professional in this field ever figures out the CPN.

The CPN? It's simply the Cost Per Nip. When we divide the admission fee for gaining entry into a topless pool area by the SGNC, we get the CPN. The lower the CPN, the higher the ANEI. But the ANEI must also be adjusted for the NIM, or Nipples In Motion, factor. Static nipples haven't nearly the entertainment value of bouncing nipples, so stripper-grade nipples involved in a titty-ball game will jack up the ANEI considerably.

The typical scene at the Sapphire pool at the Rio

Titty Ball—
A New American Sport

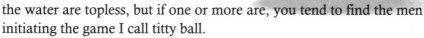

If you're not a topless-pool aficionado, allow me to explain "titty ball." Some of the American pools provide beach balls for the guests' entertainment. Typically, a topless pool has a fairly equal number of male and female guests in the water, some of whom smack the beach balls around. Not all the females in the water are topless, but if one or more are, you tend to find the men initiating the game I call titty ball.

The object of the game is to hit the ball in such a way that one of the topless females has to jump for it, thus exposing her glistening wet titties. The men keep score silently, as I believe the women don't know that a titty-ball game is in progress. They seem to believe they're simply hitting a beach ball around. But men never play a game unless it's a competition and they often high-five each other when one of them pulls off a "double McGillicuddy": a beach ball hit with such perfect timing, velocity, and angle that two topless girls leap for it simultaneously. A double McGillicuddy is an awe-inspiring thing to see. It's the titty-ball equivalent of a hole-in-one or stealing home plate.

I'm not going through all the math on this for you. Suffice it to say that I have an Excel spreadsheet set up with a macro for figuring out each pool's ANEI precisely and I've double-checked all my numbers. This is science, not guesswork.

Except, that is, for the scientific guesswork.

Here's the problem. Every American-style topless pool—the ones we really like—needs a starter, the first girl to take off her top. Once one girl starts showing her titties, the other girls look at her and say, "Hey, my tits are at least as good as hers," and tops start flying off left and right.

Fact is, most American girls have terrible body images. It doesn't matter how gorgeous their bodies are (to us guys), they feel inferior. They think their breasts are too small, or one hangs lower than the other, or the nipples aren't centered right. Talk to any American girl sometime about her boobs and you'll see what I mean. These girls all grew up playing with Barbie dolls. How do you compete with that?

Once they see other topless girls, however, they suddenly realize that the competition isn't all that great. Then they see how all the guys are now looking at the topless babe and they can't wait to get their titties in the sunshine.

If you want to time your pool visit for maximum potential topless fun, plan to arrive at around 3:30 in the afternoon. By that time, many women have been at the pool since noon, knocking down piña coladas and margaritas and mojitos and basically getting pretty damn juiced up. All it takes now is a starter to get the titty action going. The play here is to just keep buying drinks for the girls in bikinis. Think of it as an investment in your immediate future.

Some of the best topless pools are the ones where the strippers go—I identify these in my reviews. There is one exceptional "Brazilian-style" pool in Las Vegas, where you can always be sure you'll see topless girls with the highest SGNC in town. This pool, Sapphire at the Rio, has strippers from the get-go and is always worth the money. Strippers, of course, don't have the same kinds of jitters about not having Barbie-perfect tits as other girls. Even the ones who've had boob jobs look at their tits and see less-than-perfect Barbieness. But they also see other women's breasts enough to know that no girls' tits are perfect and that guys go nuts for them anyway. So stripper pools always have a starter as soon as the strippers show up.

The basic problem at most American-style pools, however, is that sometimes the strippers don't show up. So unless you bring your wife or girlfriend—and she's the kind of woman you can be sure

174

will get her nipples out into the sun before the afternoon ends—you never know for sure if a starter will get the action going. You could be at an American-style topless pool all afternoon and see nary a nipple. You'll see lots of babes in bikinis, sure, but all those entertaining nipples could be wasted. Unfortunately, despite industry standards, we can't use the Adjusted Nipple Entertainment Index with full confidence. You have to realize that the ANEI, at best, can only indicate the potential for nipple entertainment. It's up to you guys to keep the girls drinking and doing whatever you have to do to encourage one starter to make the afternoon worth the outrageous fee you paid to get in.

Also note that a number of the topless pools have specific days of the week when locals get in free. These pools don't post signs that say, "Nevada Residents Free Today." You either know this in advance, or you ask at the entrance, or you pay like everyone else. Again, one thing to remember if you live in this town and go anywhere with an

Topless-Pool Quick-Reference Guide			
CASINO	**NAME**	**STYLE**	**ANEI**
Rio	Sapphire Pool	Brazilian	9.5
Venetian	TAO Beach	American	7.0
Flamingo	GO Pool	American	6.5
Mandalay Bay	Moorea Beach Club	American	5.0
Mirage	Bare	American	5.0
Stratosphere	Beach Club 25	American	4.5
Green Valley Ranch	The Pond	American	4.0
Wynn	Sunset Pool	European	3.0
Caesars Palace	Venus Pool Club	European	1.0
Golden Nugget	The Tank	European	0.1
Encore	European Pool	European	Pending
Red Rock Resort	Cabana Club	American	Pending

admission charge—strip clubs, nightclubs, casino shows, pools—is to ask if there's a better rate for local residents. In Vegas, we take care of our own and let the tourists pay top dollar.

One final note: Most topless pools, because they're "adults only" and have full bars, have an age requirement of 21 or older.

Pool-Ratings Key

Sometimes it's tough to tell the RNC's from the CPN's. To refresh your memory, here's a quick reference to the key variables that go into determining the the best topless pools in Sin City.

RATING	DESCRIPTION
RNC: Raw Nipple Count	A count of all female nipples on display at a topless pool.
SGNC: Stripper Grade Nipple Count	A count of the female nipples on display at a topless pool that belong to women that most men would pay to see at a strip club.
CPN: Cost per Nip	Divide the admission fee for gaining entrance to a topless pool area by the SGNC to arrive at the CPN.
NIM: Nipples in Motion	A factor that increases the ANEI, due to dancing or water sports at a topless pool.
ANEI: Adjusted Nipple Entertainment Index	A topless pool rating system (scale of 0 to 10) that takes into account the SGNC, the NIM, and the CPN to arrive at a measure of entertainment value for the typical male horndog.

10

Topless Pools Reviewed

CAESARS PALACE

Name: Venus Pool Club
Phone: (702) 650-5944; (800) 634-6001
Hours: Seasonal; 9 a.m.–6 p.m., or later
Minimum Age: 21
Cover Charge: Mon.–Fri. free; Sat.–Sun., holidays, and special events $20
Amenities: Full bar, food, cabanas, day beds, and massages are available; call for prices and reservations
Category: European-style topless
Website: venuspoolclub.com

Adjusted Nipple Entertainment Index: 1.0

Caesars Palace deserves credit for starting the whole topless adult-pool trend in Las Vegas when the Venus Pool Club opened about 10 years ago, but today … Dullsville. If it was once a happening place for the in-crowd, with topless starlets flirting with Caesars' high-rolling clientele, those days appear to be long gone.

On a hot summer Sunday afternoon, for example, I viewed a total of four female nipples. They belonged to two women standing together and drinking highballs in chest-deep water. Both were in their 40s and in less-than-tip-top shape. Any guy considering paying $20 to get into this pool should know up front that it's for the rich older Europeans who stay at Caesars Palace when they come to Vegas. A few may be women who want to get sunshine on their tits without being ogled. Fine. But these are mostly just people who don't want to put up with the screaming kids in the regular pool area.

The pool itself is long, maybe 12 by 80 feet or so and shallow, sort of like a lap pool, though no one was swimming when I was there. Of the 50 or so guests in the pool area, about 15 were in the water, just relaxing around the edges. The rest were sunning on the deck. But no one was moving. Nobody came here to party.

Deck lounges in both the sun and shade and umbrella lounges were available. Pop and soft rock music at a reasonable decibel level emanated from the speakers. A Bud Light cost me $9. A menu of simple food—sandwiches, wraps, salads, etc.—had items in the $13 to $16 range. It was a comfortable area to relax in. I'll give it that much.

The tip-off that this is a European pool: There's no outrageously higher admission fee for men. That's always a bad sign.

I'm giving this pool an adjusted nipple entertainment index of 1.0, instead of 0.0, because it's always possible some hot Italian babe will show up.

Snyder says:
Rich old dudes get to see rich old ladies' titties.

ENCORE

Name: European Pool
Phone: (702) 770-7171
Hours: Seasonal; 8 a.m.–7 p.m.
Minimum Age: 21
Cover Charge: Encore and Wynn hotel guests only
Amenities: Full bar, food, cabanas, and massages are available
Category: European-style topless
Website: encorelasvegas.com

Adjusted Nipple Entertainment Index: Pending

I can only provide a cursory review of this pool. Encore opened in December 2008, so the pool hasn't been operational during the peak summer months. I did visit it in late April, shortly after it opened for the 2009 season. The weather was pleasant, but it wasn't the typical 100°+ summer heat, which no doubt contributes to a lot of decisions to shed clothing.

The pool was fairly crowded, however, on the Sunday I went, and there were even a couple of topless females present. Unfortunately, the SGNC was 0, as these were not exactly the kind of nipples I was looking for. I'll revisit this pool later in the summer to give it a fair shake and establish an ANEI rating.

Encore is a Wynn property, so I don't have my hopes up for this pool. (See my review of Wynn's topless Sunset Pool, which I did see in the heat of summer last year.) Encore simply calls this the "European Pool," and I suspect that's exactly what it will be. It's smaller but more attractive than the Wynn's. A shallow horseshoe-shaped wading/lounging pool wraps around the central bar. Palm trees surround it, with plenty of umbrella'd daybeds and lounges for guests and quite a few lounges available in shaded areas. Domestic beers are priced at $6.50, and a small menu of bar food—sandwiches, salads, and wraps—is priced from $10 to $16.

Five blackjack tables are located in the shaded bar area. Non-hotel guests may enter this area (escorted by security) to play blackjack only (no pool use allowed). All the games are dealt from six-deck shoes, with dealers hitting soft 17. Limits on four of the tables were $15-$5,000. One table had limits from $100 to $5,000. Non-hotel guests may also get into the European pool area by renting a cabana (call the number above for prices and availability).

The sound system is better than at Wynn's Sunset Pool, though there was no DJ. There's also a spa. No beach balls were provided in the pool, however, so guests just lounged around the edges. I doubt the atmosphere will change much with the heat of summer, but I'll be back to see. Watch the SinCityAdvisor. com site for updates.

Snyder says:
It's too early to tell for sure, but I don't have high hopes for this pool.

FLAMINGO

Name: GO Pool
Phone: (702) 733-3111
Hours: Seasonal; 9 a.m.–6 p.m.
Minimum Age: 21
Cover Charge: Sun.–Thurs. men, $20, Fri. and Sat. $30; ladies, free
Amenities: Full bar, food, cabanas, day beds, hookahs, and massages are available
Category: American-style topless
Website: flamingolasvegas.com

Adjusted Nipple Entertainment Index: 6.5

Flamingo's GO Pool is a locals' favorite frequented by a party crowd. A live DJ spins modern and classic rock, hip-hop, disco—whatever he feels like. The MC gets on the mike every now and then and encourages the female guests to lose their bikini tops; some surrender to his encouragement. So, this is a pool where we tip the DJ and MC. They're on our side!

More than 100 guests were in the pool area on my first weekend visit, having fun splashing around, with a lively titty-ball game in progress. Only two topless females in the pool qualified for the SGNC, but that just made the titty-ball game all the more challenging.

The Floating Stripper Pole Banned

Early in the summer of 2008, the pool had a floating stripper pole and the DJ encouraged girls to get topless and pole dance. This made the GO Pool one of the wildest topless pools in town. In August, however, the stripper pole was taken away and, according to the DJ, it's gone for good. I don't know what political machinations were behind this development, because the GO Pool guests definitely enjoyed the pole dancing. The DJ said the decision to take the pole away was due to "the law." One source tells me the pool had no entertainment license and the pole dancing was viewed as entertainment. I'm sure the Flamingo could fight this charge, since the pole dancers were just guests having fun, not being paid. Another source tells me that a guest was injured when the pole toppled and conked him on the head. Sad …

Snyder says: The MC does his damnedest to turn this pool into a "Girls Gone Wild" episode.

The MC's on Our Side

Of the 50 or so women in the GO Pool area on my last weekend visit, only six were topless and of these, only three figured into the SGNC. But lots of cute girls were wearing bikinis, and the shamelessly juvenile attitude of the MC cracks me up. For example, after the DJ played Katy Perry's "I Kissed a Girl," the MC couldn't help but get on the mike and start encouraging the girls in the pool to start kissing each other. (Hey, if you can't pole dance …) So the MC continues to do whatever he can to turn the pool into an episode of "Girls Gone Wild" and even without the stripper pole, I still like the GO Pool.

I also love those cute pink-and-black-lingerie bikinis the cocktail servers wear at this pool. A man could easily while away the afternoon just kicking

Holly Madison was on hand to kick-off the 2009 pool season at GO

back with a margarita and watching the waitresses walk around in the sunshine.

The pool is kidney-shaped and surrounded by palm trees and statues of giant flamingos on pedestals, spitting (retching?) streams of water into the pool. It's not difficult to come by deck lounges in the shade, even when the pool is crowded.

A beer here is $6. There's also an inexpensive menu of burgers, dogs, sandwiches, pizza, salads, and wraps, reasonably priced from $7 to $12. You can also rent a poolside hookah if you're into that scene and poolside massage is available.

On Mondays, the GO Pool has a "Relapse Party," free for locals. It's non-topless, with a sign posted to that effect at the entrance. I've heard that the girls sometimes disregard the sign and get topless on Mondays anyway, though on my last Monday visit, no nipples were in sight. Big crowd, hot sunny day, lots of cute girls in bikinis, but no starter. I'm basing the adjusted nipple entertainment index on a typical topless weekend.

The GO Pool at the Flamingo

GOLDEN NUGGET

Name: The Tank
Phone: (702) 385-7111; (800) 946-5336
Hours: Seasonal; 10 a.m.–5 p.m.
Minimum Age: Upper deck, 21
Cover Charge: Hotel guests, free; non-hotel guests, adults $20, children $15
Amenities: 2 full bars, food, cabanas, and day beds are available; call for prices and reservations
Category: European-style topless
Website: goldennugget.com

Adjusted Nipple Entertainment Index: 0.1

The Tank is not a topless pool.

So what are we doing here?

We're here because the Golden Nugget provides a topless adults-only sunning area on a hidden upper deck of the regular pool area. But if you've already noticed that men don't pay more than women to be admitted to this pool, you might presume it's just another European-style pool where you probably won't get much topless entertainment.

If you're not too disappointed in the dearth of nipples here and you can put up with all of the ankle biters, this has got to be one of the coolest pools in Vegas. It's big and has two waterfalls, plus a giant saltwater fish tank right in the middle of it, so you can swim with the sharks. In addition, a great waterslide starts up on the third deck and becomes a clear tube on the way down that goes right through the fish tank. There are also lots of cute girls in bikinis, but even more kids, who make a racket that can be heard over the top of the loud rock, funk, and hip-hop music. This is like a family pool-party scene and it's fun for all. I visited The Tank on a hot Saturday afternoon when it was packed, but despite the crowd, I had no trouble finding a deck chair in the shade.

Inexpensive food—sandwiches, wraps, burgers, salads, nachos, etc.—is served by waitresses. Prices range from $6.99 for a hot dog to $11.99 for a chicken Caesar salad. There are also two full bars and cocktail servers. A domestic beer is $6.

The topless area is on the third level, past the entrance to the waterslide and cabanas. It's a small area around the last corner, with nine deck lounges and nothing else. A posted sign says, "Adults Only." Two people were in the area when I arrived, a young guy and his girl. She was topless, but I couldn't actually see her nipples, because she and her boyfriend were sharing a deck lounge, locked in a passionate embrace. I'm absolutely certain she had stripper-grade nipples, as she was in her early twenties and cute as hell from the back in her little bikini bottom. But the topless deck area is so small and so far out of the way, I doubt even cocktail or food service makes it up there, and topless girls don't have a pool or even a spa to go into. Sorry, no titty ball. Have fun on the waterslide.

Snyder says:
Topless?
What topless?
I'm here for the
waterslide!

The Tank at the Golden Nugget

GREEN VALLEY RANCH

Name: The Pond
Phone: (702) 617-7777; (866) 782-9487
Hours: Seasonal; 11 a.m.–7 p.m.; after Labor day 11 a.m.–6 p.m.
Minimum Age: 21
Cover Charge: None
Amenities: Full bar, food, cabanas, and day beds are available
Category: American-style topless
Website: greenvalleyranchresort.com

Adjusted Nipple Entertainment Index: 4.0

Okay, you're confused. Green Valley Ranch's topless pool, The Pond, doesn't have a higher price for men (in fact, it's free to the public!), yet I'm categorizing it as an "American-style" topless pool. How can this be?

This place is different. GVR is a Station casino and caters to locals—in this case, the residents of Henderson where GVR is located. As it turns out, quite a few Las Vegas strippers live in Henderson. Green Valley Ranch lets them (and the general public) into the topless Pond for free (the main pool, the sand-bottom Beach, is for hotel guests or cabana renters only). So on days when the dancers want to work on their tans, this pool has a good bunch of starters and the party gets pretty wild.

The pool itself is small and square with a filmy curtain of a waterfall pouring into it on one end. There are cabanas and day beds for rent and lots of deck lounges for free, but not a lot of shade available—unless you pay for it. At the full bar, a domestic beer is $7.

The food menu is good—beyond just bar food. Sandwiches, tacos, salads, and wraps are mostly priced in the $10-$15 range. Appetizers include lobster quesadillas and grilled chicken satay (both of which I've tried and recommend).

If you're headed to The Pond to see topless girls, watch for the action to begin later in the afternoon when the margaritas take hold.

Again, it's a catch-as-catch-can situation. If no starters show up, you may just have to suffer through the sight of the girls in skimpy bikinis dancing to the hip-hop, rock, and metal the DJ spins. I can think of worse tortures, especially when it's free to get in.

Snyder says:
It's always free and the local strippers like it (so I hear ...).

The Pond at Green Valley Ranch

187

MANDALAY BAY

Name: Moorea Beach Club
Phone: (702) 632-7777; (800) 632-7000
Hours: Seasonal; 8 a.m.–5 p.m., or later
Minimum Age: 21
Cover Charge: Sun.–Thurs. men, $40, Fri. and Sat. $50; ladies, $10
Amenities: Full bar, food, day beds, opium beds, massages, and pavilions are available; call for prices and reservations
Category: American-style topless
Website: mandalaybay.com

Adjusted Nipple Entertainment Index: 5.0

Mandalay Bay's Moorea Beach Club is open to everyone, though it'll cost you $40 to $50 to get in if you're a guy, $10 if you're a woman.

That tells us that this is an American-style topless pool. Ah yes. They expect a good titty show, so the guys have to pay for it.

The problem is that this pool isn't open to the general public, so it never attracts the local strippers. Don't underestimate the effect of the local stripper population on the topless pool scene. Thousands of strippers live in Vegas and most feel that tan lines are unattractive. They're out there looking for topless pools and this one's off limits.

I suspect MBay feels it can charge guys more simply because the casino attracts a young crowd. This is a hip place with some of the hottest nightclubs in town—the House of Blues, rumjungle, the Eyecandy Sound Lounge, and the Mix Lounge—there's even a tattoo parlor on the premises. Since it aims for and gets a hip young crowd, some of the babes in the pool will get topless, so the guys have to pay for the show.

On a hot weekend afternoon in the summer, you'll find the pool fairly crowded—maybe 100 guests on average, about half men and half women, mostly in their 20s and 30s. Perhaps a quarter of the female guests will be topless—relaxing in the long thin arc-shaped pool, sitting in one of the two spas, or sunning on the deck. On a typical day, about half the topless women would figure into the SGNC. Unfortu-

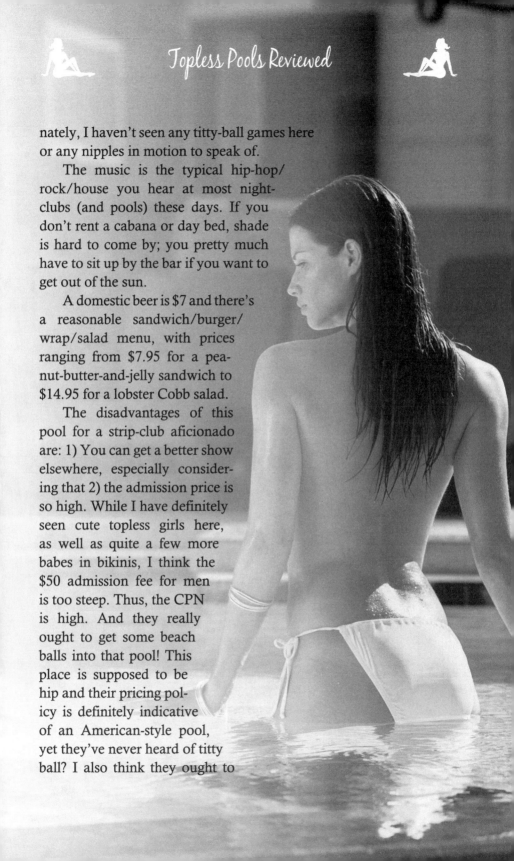

nately, I haven't seen any titty-ball games here or any nipples in motion to speak of.

The music is the typical hip-hop/rock/house you hear at most nightclubs (and pools) these days. If you don't rent a cabana or day bed, shade is hard to come by; you pretty much have to sit up by the bar if you want to get out of the sun.

A domestic beer is $7 and there's a reasonable sandwich/burger/wrap/salad menu, with prices ranging from $7.95 for a pea-nut-butter-and-jelly sandwich to $14.95 for a lobster Cobb salad.

The disadvantages of this pool for a strip-club aficionado are: 1) You can get a better show elsewhere, especially consider-ing that 2) the admission price is so high. While I have definitely seen cute topless girls here, as well as quite a few more babes in bikinis, I think the $50 admission fee for men is too steep. Thus, the CPN is high. And they really ought to get some beach balls into that pool! This place is supposed to be hip and their pricing pol-icy is definitely indicative of an American-style pool, yet they've never heard of titty ball? I also think they ought to make a few more umbrellas available out in the deck lounge areas. That Vegas sun is hot. In any case, even if I had a room at Mandalay Bay, I probably wouldn't pay fifty bucks to go to this pool, with so many better topless pools around for less.

Snyder says: The admission fee for men makes the CPN (Cost Per Nip) too high.

MIRAGE

Name: Bare Pool Lounge
Phone: (702) 791-7442; (800) 627-6667
Hours: Seasonal; 11 a.m.–7 p.m.
Minimum Age: 21
Cover Charge: Sun.–Thurs. men, $20, women, $10; Fri. and Sat. men, $40, women, $20; Thurs. and Sun. locals, free with valid ID
Amenities: Full bar, food, cabanas, day beds, and massages are available
Category: European-style, top optional
Website: mirage.com

Adjusted Nipple Entertainment Index: 5.0

Mirage promotes this pool with a definite emphasis on topless. Numerous big posters around the casino, and even highway billboards, show a topless babe from the back, with the slogan: "Bare: Lose the Tan Line." And since men are charged twice as much as women for admission, I was expecting a pretty good party atmosphere. But sometimes a place can be just too elegant for its own good. The mood here is more like an aristocratic tea party than a beer bash.

Out of about 100 guests in the pool area the weekday afternoon I was there, 50 or so were women, 10 were topless, and eight of them—a pretty high percentage—figured into the SGNC. Still, it wasn't much of a party scene—most guests were just relaxing in the pool or spa or sunning on the deck. No titty ball. No nipples in motion.

This is another pool that allows topless sunbathing during the week, but reportedly not on the weekends. A buddy who went on a Sunday afternoon said he found lots of cute topless girls and a pretty wild scene, but when I followed up with a visit on a hot August day (107°F) the following weekend, there wasn't a topless girl in sight. Maybe it's because the $40 weekend cover charge ($20 for women) is too steep. If you do go on a weekend, try Sunday, when locals get in for free.

The pool itself is small and rectangular, about 40 by 15 feet. A domestic beer will cost you $9 at the full bar. The food service consists of typical pizzas, salads, and sandwiches, with most items in the $15 to $20 range—again, a bit steep.

If you're a local, this pool is also free on either Wednesdays or Thursdays (they experimented with both days during the summer of 2008), so I guess it's worth a shot if you can get in *gratis*. I just don't think this pool is worth the price, given the other less-expensive options in town.

Snyder says:
More like an aristocratic tea party than a beer bash.

Topless Pools Reviewed

RED ROCK RESORT

Name: Cherry Cabana Club
Phone: (702) 797-7777
Hours: Seasonal; 10 a.m.–7 p.m.
Minimum Age: 21
Cover Charge: Free for all (may change as season progresses)
Amenities: Full bar, cabanas, and day beds available
Category: American-style topless
Website: redrockresort.com

Adjusted Nipple Entertainment Index: Pending

The Cherry Cabana Club at the Red Rock Resort recently became Las Vegas' 10th topless pool that's accessible to the public. The Red Rock Resort has been open for about five years, but this pool didn't become topless until August 2008, a month before it shut down for the season. I didn't even hear about it until it was closed. So I didn't get to see it last summer when I did my pool surveys. The pool recently re-opened and I did get to see it in operation, though in mid-April. There were no topless girls the afternoon I was there, but I can't assign this pool an ANEI rating until later in the summer when the weather's hot and the pools are in full swing.

The Cabana Club is accessible through a gate from the regular pool area. I'm rating it as American-style, however, since last year, when there was a $30 cover charge, local ladies always got in for free. This is exactly the kind of pool the Vegas stripper population is looking for and it's the only one of its kind on the west side of town in the Summerlin area. At present (April 2009), there is no cover charge for anyone, though you must be 21 and show ID to gain admittance.

The pool itself is shallow and arc-shaped with a sitting ledge all the way around, like a large hot tub, great for lounging. Sadly, no beach balls were provided to guests. Hopefully, this will change. The pool area is upscale and attractive, with palm trees on one side. In the evening hours, the area is open to guests of the Cherry nightclub, which caters to a hip young singles crowd. On the weekends, there's a DJ.

A domestic beer costs $8, and there is a pretty extensive menu of bar food—burgers, salads, sandwiches, etc., most in the $10-$15 range. The "Cherry Retreat" starts on May 10. On Sunday and Monday, guests will get a special hotel rate and a pool party on Sunday, VIP bowling on Monday, then a midnight "Sips & Dips" pool party.

Red Rock Resort is trying hard to become the Summerlin party headquarters. The regular pool area is free to all every Saturday night for its "Rhythms of the Night" party, which features a DJ, live percussion, dancers, etc. And beginning June 5, every Friday night will also be free for all with live jazz.

I have my hopes up for the Cherry Cabana Club. Nice setting, good location, no cover for ladies (or anyone right now!), just add beach balls and stir. C'mon, Red Rock! Get them beach balls!

Snyder says:
Just add beach balls and stir …

RIO

Name: Sapphire Pool
Phone: (702) 777-7709; (800)
Hours: Seasonal; 10 a.m.–6 p.m.
Cover Charge: Men, Mon.–Fri. $30, ladies, $10; men, Sat.–Sun. $50, ladies, $10; men, holidays $60, ladies, $10
Amenities: No bar, but cocktail service is excellent; no food service, but food can be brought in from the Rio's regular pool snack bar; cabanas, and day beds available
Category: Brazilian-style topless
Website: rio.com

Adjusted Nipple Entertainment Index: 9.5

Okay, so I pay my $50 weekend admission fee, walk into the Sapphire Pool area, and immediately bump into two topless babes standing on the deck in thong bikini bottoms. The girl in the tiger-striped thong has her arms stretched over her head, while the other is rubbing suntan lotion on Tiger Girl's back.

Time to locate a deck lounge. This place looks promising.

If you've ever tried to imagine the ideal topless pool scene, one that you probably thought could only exist in your fantasies, the Sapphire Pool at the Rio probably comes pretty close.

What's going on here? Sapphire, Las Vegas' largest gentlemen's club, leases the private pool area from the Rio and makes it available to the Sapphire dancers at no charge. The dancers, who can swim and sunbathe topless, take advantage of this in droves.

Further enhancing the visual delight of all those topless beauties is the stunning pool landscaping. The pool itself is small and irregularly shaped, but three waterfalls flow into it from a rock formation at one side, with a thick foliage of palm trees all around. It's like a tropical oasis.

Snyder says:
Imagine a topless
pool that could
only exist in your
fantasies ...

The Highest Stripper Grade Nipple Count—Guaranteed!

With a DJ spinning hip-hop and top 40 tunes, this is another topless pool with a party atmosphere, similar to Flamingo's GO Pool or Venetian's TAO Beach, but with a much higher percentage of topless girls and just about all of them stripper grade, since most—if not all—are actual strippers. They splash around in the water and play titty ball with whatever guys are brave enough to get in there with them. They stand on the decks and rub sunscreen on each other. They stretch out on the deck chairs and on floating inflated rafts in the pool. Deck lounges are available in both sun and shade. But to hell with that! It's hard not to get in the water and mingle with the fauna.

You get to the Sapphire Pool by walking through the Rio's regular pool area. A domestic beer is $7, but when I paid my entry fee, I got a free-drink coupon. I don't know if you always get the free drink with admission, but this year, the entry fee for local men with ID is half-price! Finally, a stimulus package I can believe in!

About 80 guests were in the pool area on the Sunday afternoon I was there, about half men and half women. Most of the crowd was young—20s and 30s—and most of the women were topless. The SGNC at this pool was 46 on the day I was there, and even with that $50 cover charge, the CPN was only $1.09. And a good portion of those stripper grade nipples were NIMs. That's why the ANEI is so high.

If you like the idea of splashing around with some cute young topless girls, or just lying back with a brewski and watching them splash around, this is the place. About the only thing that could make this pool even better than it is would be if they could get that retired floating stripper pole from Flamingo's GO Pool and start putting it to good use.

[Warning to young guys: If you get turned on easily by the sight of dripping wet babes in little thongs, you may have to strap it down inside your trunks or you'll be pitching a tent in your deck chair.]

STRATOSPHERE

Name: Beach Club 25
Phone: (702) 380-7777; (800) 998-6937
Hours: Seasonal; 10 a.m.–6 p.m.
Minimum Age: 21
Cover Charge: Hotel guests, $10; non-hotel guests, $20; ladies, free
Amenities: Full bar, no food service, ping-pong table for guest use at no charge
Category: American-style topless
Website: stratospherehotel.com

Adjusted Nipple Entertainment Index: 4.5

I visited the Stratosphere's topless pool on a very hot weekend day in the mid-afternoon. Only about 40 people were in the pool area, but half of them were in the water playing titty ball with the single topless girl in the pool who qualified for the SGNC. That girl is the reason the Strat's pool gets as high of an ANEI rating as it does. (Of the six topless females in the pool area, only three qualified for the SGNC.)

The Strat's topless pool is called Beach Club 25, presumably because it's located on the 25th floor. Technically, there isn't a 25th floor at the Stratosphere where the pool is located. You take the elevator to the 24th floor, then walk up a flight of stairs to the pool on the roof. You get some fabulous views of Las Vegas on two sides. (Note: From the casino level, take the World II elevators located next to Fellini's Italian Restaurant and you'll come out on the 24th floor right beside the stairway that leads to the pool. Other elevators to the 24th floor and other stairways on the 24th floor don't go to the rooftop pool, so just take the World II elevators and you'll see the sign for the Beach Club 25 stairway.)

The pool itself is rectangular, about 20 by 50 feet, and a volleyball net is set up across the center to encourage titty ball. There's also a ping-pong table in the bar area that anyone can use. Shade is available both up by the bar and on the deck. A domestic beer costs only $5.25.

When I was there, the bartender was also the DJ, spinning hip-hop and modern rock.

This pool is really cool because of the fantastic views, but the Strat just isn't doing much to promote it. For a hot Saturday afternoon, the crowd was pretty sparse. I don't think the locals know about it. With ladies getting free admission and better drink prices than most of the other pools, you'd think this pool would be a lot more popular. Why don't you help make it so.

Snyder says: Cool pool, great view, an undiscovered gem.

VENETIAN

Name: TAO Beach
Phone: (702) 388-8588; (877) 883-6423
Hours: Seasonal; Mon.–Thurs. 10 a.m.–sunset; Fri. and Sat. 10 a.m.–nightclub closing; Sun. 10 a.m.–10 p.m. (no public admission after 6 p.m.)
Minimum Age: 21
Cover Charge: Mon.–Thurs. free; Fri.–Sun. $30
Amenities: Full bar, food, cabanas, and massages are available
Category: American-style topless Mon.–Fri. only
Website: taolasvegas.com

Adjusted Nipple Entertainment Index: 7.0

Okay, your mission—should you choose to accept it—is to gain entrance to the TAO Beach Pool. And believe me, that's easier said than done. This pool suffers from being a bit too popular with the club set. If you're not a Venetian hotel guest with a key, you have to go to the TAO Beach podium on the second floor of the Venetian, up the escalator by the Apothecary shop, where a host decides whether or not you make the grade. If so, he escorts you past the guard to the elevator you take to get to the pool.

So getting past this host is like getting into a popular nightclub where the doorman decides who gets to go in based on how hip they're dressed. Sexy young babes always get in. Any guy who looks like a horndog showing up because he read this book will likely be turned away.

The first thing this host asks you is if you have a reservation. With a cabana reserved, obviously, you get in. If not, you'll be asked if you're on the guest list. The guest list? Oh, yes, this pool is very popular with celebrities (bands I never heard of, TV personalities I never heard of, movie stars I never heard of) who rent cabanas and make the scene, so if you're part of one of the entourages, you're in.

Getting Past the Dork Detectors

Here are a few tips on getting into this pool when you have no Venetian room key, you have no reservation, and you're not on a guest list:

1) Go early. The more crowded the pool is, the more difficult it is to get in.

2) Don't look like a dork. If you can't help it because you are, in fact, a dork, at least look like a rich hip dork. Wear cool shades and beach clothes like you fully expect to get in. A tattoo and a few piercings might help. If you're losing your hair, shave your head. Finally, shave your chest. Hip guys today are all walking around the pools with chest stubble. You've got to look like you belong.

3) Go with a girl. Unescorted guys are turned away a lot quicker than men accom-

Snyder says:
Shave your chest if you have to—this pool's worth it!

TAO Beach gets crowded on the weekends.

panied by women. Of course, if you had a woman, you probably wouldn't be going to a topless pool.

4) Tip the podium host, with the amount of your tip based on the difficulty level of your getting in. If you're young, good-looking, tattooed, pierced, and you've got chest stubble, five bucks might do the trick. If you're hopelessly uncool, it might take a twenty. Note, however, that this tip only gets you onto the elevator to the fourth floor so you can enter the regular pool area. It doesn't get you all the way to TAO Beach.

Once you get into the regular pool area, just follow the signs to TAO Beach, where you'll find a line of people just like you who somehow managed to get this far and now must convince yet another dork detector that they're cool enough to party with B-movie extras and rappers' roadies. How do you get past this final obstacle? Follow the exact same four tips described above. Go early. Don't be a dork. Go with a girl. And if all else fails, bribe your way in.

TAO Beach is another topless pool where guys pay the same admission fee as women, but I'm categorizing it as American-style anyway. Why? Because it's so damn hip, they've got policies and procedures in place that make it rock, so strippers come here to get a tan.

The pool is located on the roof of the TAO nightclub. On weekday afternoons, it's open to the public with free admission, which makes it very popular. Admission fees are charged on weekends and evenings, when the pool party becomes an extension of the TAO nightclub. I don't cover the TAO nightclub scene, because there are no topless girls there. All of my comments below apply to the pool, during daylight hours only.

TAO Beach on the Weekend

Let's start with the weekend when you have to pay to get in. Officially, topless sunbathing is verboten, but rumor has it that sometimes a starter shows up and if no one complains, the babes start doffing their tops. To see if there was any truth to the rumor, I went on a very crowded Sunday afternoon and spent almost four hours there. It was

104° and by three o'clock, all those margaritas and mojitos had the crowd loosened up to the point where they were dancing in the pool, on the decks, in and around the spa—100 hot babes in string bikinis and dudes with no body hair boogying like there was no tomorrow. But nary a nipple in sight (a female nipple, that is). No starters. I think that $30 weekend cover tends to put off a lot of the strippers who know where the free topless pools are.

So the weekend party is hit or miss as far as the RNC. But TAO Beach still rocks. Even if the girls don't shed their tops, I just want to be there at three o'clock in the afternoon when those mojitos kick in and all those babes start dancing. This is better than an Annette Funicello movie!

If you're trying to pick up a girl and don't succeed at this pool party, you've got some serious social problems. Due to that no-uncool-guys-without-a-girl admission policy, the girls outnumber the boys by a wide margin and they're all getting plastered. I'm just glad I'm married and no longer have to go through all that hooking-up crap. (Sigh.)

Weekdays Rock!

But if you want guaranteed topless, go on a weekday and you don't even have to pay to get in (assuming you can get past the dork detectors). I went on a hot Thursday afternoon and found about 80 people, mostly young and good-looking. Lots of bikinis. A dozen girls were topless and eight of them were stripper grade.

TAO Beach understands titty ball like no other topless pool in town. They have a generous supply of about two dozen beach balls in the pool, and those balls start flying right away. The NIM factor is big here. The small shallow pool is perfectly designed to encourage this fast-growing sport. And be sure to check out the reclining Buddha overlooking the spa, where the girls like to go to take pictures of each other with their digital cameras. I like sitting up by the bar and watching them pose.

The DJ plays mostly hip-hop and house music and cranks up the volume as the afternoon wears on. There's shade in the bar area and under a few umbrella lounges, but it's not easy to come by with the crowds that show up.

There's a full bar. A domestic beer is $9. The grill menu has burgers, salads, and lots of satays. Prices run from $9 for a hot dog to $27 for a big mixed-satay plate. If you want a greater selection of food choices, you can go outside the TAO Beach area to the Venetian's regular pool area, where you'll find an outdoor restaurant called Riva, a Wolfgang Puck eatery. You can come and go from TAO Beach to the regular pool area, so long as you wear the wristband you get when you first enter.

Technically, whether topless or not, TAO Beach is a singles club where young people in Vegas go to find someone to get laid. It's a party atmosphere start to finish. But if all you're going for is to ogle the girls, you won't be disappointed.

TAO Beach brings in big-name DJs, such as Samantha Ronson here.

WYNN

Name: Sunset Pool
Phone: (702) 770-7000; (866) 770-7108
Hours: Seasonal; 8 a.m.–8 p.m.
Minimum Age: 21
Cover Charge: Hotel guests only, free
Amenities: Full bar, food, cabanas, and massages are available
Category: European-style topless
Website: wynnlasvegas.com

Adjusted Nipple Entertainment Index: 3.0

I checked this pool numerous times on weekdays and weekends. There were always topless women there and almost every one I saw was young and good-looking—definitely stripper grade. But alas, the pool's a snooze.

The topless women in the water mostly stayed submerged from the chest down. There were no titty-ball games—nor even any hope of one starting—because there were no beach balls. Someone needs to inform the entertainment director at Wynn that it's the job of pool management to supply the beach balls. Tourists don't come to Vegas with their own beach balls. The pool must provide them. All those wet titties wasted.

Gorgeous topless women were also lounging in the deck areas, but even as the afternoons wore on and the mojitos had to be having an effect out in that burning Vegas sun, the mickey-mouse music system precluded any spontaneous dancing in the deck areas. The DJ is off on the lawn over in the far corner of the deck area, with speakers set up beside him, but no other speakers in the Sunset Pool area. If you're not close to the DJ booth, the pop, classic rock, and soft rock he plays hardly disturbs the air. This is a huge outdoor area and the DJ has what amounts to a modest home-stereo system, which he doesn't crank up.

You come this pool to catch an afternoon nap in the sun, not to party. And if you're not staying at the Wynn, forget about coming here at all, because the Sunset pool is open only to Wynn's hotel guests. [Tip to voyeurs: If you stay at either the Wynn or Encore, be sure to request a room with a pool view. Most have a view of the topless pool as well. Don't forget to bring your binocs!]

The Sunset pool is located behind the Cabana Bar at the far end of Wynn's regular pool area. It's large and rectangular, surrounded by umbrellaed day beds that must be reserved. But hundreds of free deck lounges are available. Almost all are in the full sun during midsummer, but in the late summer, when the sun isn't so directly overhead, shaded lounges are available on the far side of the pool. Otherwise, if you want shade, you have to sit in the bar area.

Snyder says:
No titty ball, no dancing, good for a summer snooze ...

A domestic beer is $6.50 and most imports are only $7. The menu consists of typical bar food, mostly sandwiches and salads, priced from $10 to $12. A shrimp cocktail is $16.

On a hot weekday, I found about 40 people in the Sunset Pool area, a very sparse crowd given its size. On a hot Saturday afternoon, both the regular pool and the Sunset Pool areas were very crowded, with at least 150 people in the Sunset Pool area, many in the water.

If you're into relaxing, you'll probably prefer the ambience at the Sunset Pool to the blaring hip-hop so common at many topless pools in Las Vegas. Wynn isn't trying to compete with those, but simply wants to provide guests with a comfortable environment where women can be topless if they wish. This is just a nice pool, not a playground or a singles pickup scene.

Most interesting about this pool is that just about every topless girl I saw was stripper grade. I guess the rich dudes who stay at Wynn just attract hot women. For a European-style pool open to hotel guests only, with no beach balls and a bad sound system, this pool still gets an ANEI of 3.0.

Still, from my perspective, this is European-style in the worst sense of the word. If you're coming to Vegas looking for a titty show, stay at the Venetian and go to TAO Beach, where the music rocks and the beach balls are plentiful.

Part Three

Nightclubs and Casino Shows

11

Overview of the Nightclubs

In this chapter I don't rate nightclubs the way I do strip clubs, or casino shows, or topless pools—that is, on any sort of an erotic scale or dancer quality or nipple count, etc. I'm interested in nightclubs that purport to offer some kind of entertainment that could be construed as eroticism which is to say, where a clubgoer might expect to see female performers in skimpy outfits. But even the nightclubs with the sexiest shows are more geared to customers who want to drink, dance, and socialize with potential sex partners than they are to customers mostly interested in seeing a good show.

It wasn't easy choosing which clubs to include and exclude. Mandalay Bay's rumjungle has girls in bustiers, stockings, and garter belts dancing out in front of the entrance to the club. Inside, there are similarly dressed go-go dancers in cages overhead. But that's it. Cage dancers. Is rumjungle reviewed? Nah. The cage dancers are too far away to watch easily. They don't have much room to dance. And it's not much of a show. In my book, rumjungle is just a drinking and pick-up bar.

Four of the five nightclubs I chose to review have some type of entertainment advertised or promoted as a sexy show. The Playboy Club, however, I reviewed simply because the name "Playboy" has been so long associated with beautiful naked girls that a visitor to Las Vegas might be led to believe that some kind of sexy show goes on up there.

12

Nightclubs Reviewed

CATHOUSE
Luxor
3900 Las Vegas Blvd. S., Las Vegas

Phone: (702) 262-4228; (877) 333-9291
Hours: Restaurant 6 p.m.–11 p.m.; Nightclub Mon., Thurs.–Sat. 10:30 p.m.–4 a.m., Wed. 1 a.m.–4 a.m.
Minimum Age: 21
Cover Charge: Men, $30; ladies, $20; free with dinner, see description
Table Reservations: Recommended
Full Bar: Yes
Food: Yes; till 11 p.m. only
Dress Code: Stylish
Website: cathouselv.com

I had high hopes for Cathouse. When I asked the doorman what the place was like, he said it was "similar to Ivan Kane's Forty Deuce," a nightclub that used to be at Mandalay Bay that had a great burlesque show that I'd seen numerous times. I also found information on various websites about Cathouse's "Coquettes," described as dancers who not only perform choreographed routines on stage, but circulate in the audience to "create an interactive theater feel." Sexy photos of the

Coquettes online are very enticing. A number of websites claim that Cathouse searched the world for these very special dancers.

The four Coquettes, clad in the Cathouse line of lingerie (which is for sale), dance on two tiny stages about once an hour. Some seem to know a few stripper moves, though the stages aren't really big enough for them to move much. All are young and good-looking and have great bodies. But their routines aren't special enough to go out of your way for. I'd rate them as about as sexy as the "bevertainers" at the Rio, cocktail servers who also perform on platforms around the casino. And that's not a put-down. I like the bevertainers. I often stop to watch them. But I found the Cathouse show disappointing after the hype. Ivan Kane's Forty Deuce it's not.

Snyder Says: A typical touristy nightclub scene with lots of strangers trying to deliver pick-up lines.

The Cathouse waitresses also wear cute sexy outfits composed of things like bustiers and stockings with garters, which I assume are official Cathouse lingerie.

But Mostly, It's a Pick-up Bar

The crowd—mostly single visitors in their 20s and 30s—doesn't seem to quite know what to do with itself. A few try dancing on the small dance floor. Most just stand around talking and drinking with whomever they came in with. I assume those who didn't come with a significant other are looking to hook up. This is just a typical touristy nightclub scene with lots of strangers eyeing each other

Nightclubs Reviewed

uncomfortably and trying to get up the nerve to approach someone.

Most nights up until about 11 p.m., Cathouse is just a restaurant with standard steakhouse fare and prices. A New York steak is $43 and a surf 'n' turf will run you $70. On Tuesday, Thursday, and Sunday, Cathouse closes around midnight, when the last of the diners have departed. But on Monday, Wednesday, Friday, and Saturday nights, it stays open as a nightclub until 4 a.m. There's no cover charge before 11 p.m. and you don't have to order dinner even if you come early, but there is no entertainment during the restaurant hours. A beer is $7 and mixed drinks are about $12 at the full bar. There is an old-fashioned bordello theme to the décor. The walls leading into the restaurant are covered with risqué black-and-white photos of nudes, mostly from an earlier era when such photos would have been considered shocking.

The night I went, the restaurant area was closed for a private party, but the main club upstairs was open to the public. This room has a bar and two small stages.

To sum up, if you're looking for anything resembling a strip-club expericnce, this ain't it. The waitresses and Coquettes are sexy in their lingerie ensembles, but this is a nightclub, not a show, and a so-so nightclub at that. Your chances of hooking up here are a lot better than in a strip club, but your chances of getting turned on by the entertainment are just about zip.

Nightclubs Reviewed

PLAYBOY CLUB
Palms
4321 W. Flamingo Rd., Las Vegas

Phone: (702) 942-6832; (866) 942-7770
Hours: 8 p.m.–4 a.m.
Minimum Age: 21
Cover Charge: Sun.–Thurs. before 10 p.m. $10, after 10 p.m. $20;
Fri. and Sat. $40
Table Reservations: Recommended
Full Bar: Yes
Food: No
Dress Code: Upscale club wear, no athletic wear, ballcaps, tennis
shoes, shorts, or flip-flops
Website: n9negroup.com

The Playboy Club at the Palms, located on the 52nd floor, is basically a gambling pit with a nice view of Las Vegas. It has nine blackjack tables ($25 minimum) and one roulette wheel, plus some Playboy-branded slot machines. If you don't reserve a table (which will cost you, depending on the size of your party, bottle service, etc.), you'll find no comfortable seating except at a blackjack table. You can also perch on a stool at the bar, where a domestic beer runs you $7, and play video poker.

The Palms has the unique honor of housing the only Playboy Club in the world. At one time, you could find a Playboy Club in just about every major city in the U.S., and many in Europe—about three dozen in all—but the last U.S. club closed 20 years ago as entertainment tastes changed.

The only reason I'm even reviewing the Playboy Club is because the name Playboy has been associated for so long with hot naked babes and it's been so many years since a Playboy Club has been in operation that many guys under the age of 40 might not even know that a Playboy Club was historically just a swank nightclub with top-name performers. None of them ever had strippers, topless waitresses, or any other kind of sexy entertainment—unless, of course, you think Bob

Hope and Mel Tormé were sexy. This one differs from the old clubs in that it has blackjack tables instead of Mel Tormé. There is no live entertainment in the Palms' Playboy Club, just recorded music, and all the bunnies do is deal blackjack and roulette or serve cocktails.

The bunny outfits worn by the cocktail waitresses—with their strapless push-up tops, cinched waistlines, high-cut thighs, and the signature bunny ears and cottontails—were considered risqué when the first Playboy Club opened in Chicago in 1960. Today, they're more camp than vamp. The Palms' bunny suits are an updated version by designer Roberto Cavalli, but to me, they look exactly like the classic bunny duds of old. I think this Cavalli dude pulled a fast one on Hef if he

Snyder Says:
Just a blackjack pit with bunnies.

charged him much for this "new" design. (I think maybe the waistlines aren't cinched as tightly as they used to be, but that's the only difference I could see.)

If you want to get into the Playboy Club, it'll cost you $20 (or $40 on the weekends), but that also gets you into the Palms' other nightclubs—Moon, Ghostbar, and Rain. I've never visited Moon or Rain, but Ghostbar is a high-tech lounge on the 55th floor with a sweeping view of Las Vegas from the outdoor deck.

I can't recommend the Playboy Club for guys looking for sexy entertainment. You might find it worth looking at if you're out clubbing and you want to visit the Palms' other nightclubs or if you're willing to pay $20 to lose your paycheck to a bunny dealer as opposed to a dealer in any one of the Palms' blackjack pits down in the main casino. But she won't take her top off or give you a lap dance no matter how much you lose.

PUSSYCAT DOLLS LOUNGE
Caesars Palace
3570 S. Las Vegas Blvd., Las Vegas

Phone: (702) 212-8806; (800) 634-6601
Hours: Tues., Thurs.–Sat. 10 p.m.–4 a.m.
Minimum Age: 21
Cover Charge: Men, $30; ladies, $20
Table Reservations: Recommended
Full Bar: Yes
Food: No
Dress Code: No sneakers, sandals, or cut-offs
Website: pcdlounge.com

The Pussycat Dolls are essentially a lingerie-clad dance troupe. They wear corsets, garter belts, and black-mesh stockings, fronted by a singer who belts out torch songs, rock 'n' roll hits, and jazz classics. I like all the music they use in their act. The singer, Jeannie Princeton, has a great voice. She sings the Pussycat Dolls' 2005 hit song (with Busta Rhymes), "Dontcha," plus such songs as Jimi Hendrix's "Foxy Lady," Led Zeppelin's "Whole Lotta Love," and Peggy Lee's old classic "Fever." The dancers are talented and they use lots of stripper moves and do some sexy posing. And, even though they always leave their tops and bottoms on, they're sexy and fun to watch. A cute striptease number takes place in an oversized champagne glass. A girl in lingerie swings overhead for no apparent purpose. I like the Pussycat Dolls.

What I don't like is that the Pussycat Dolls' Theater is inside the Pure nightclub. So even if your only interest is the Pussycat Dolls, you have to first pay the $30 cover charge to get into Pure. Then you have to pay an additional $5 to get into the Pussycat Dolls Theater. So it's a $35 cover charge, even for locals.

The second problem with this show is that, because it's inside the Pure nightclub, the line to get in is incredibly long. In fact, on busy nights there are three lines—one for VIPs on the guest list, one for women only, and one for the general public. Needless to say, the general public's line is the long one. Can you tip your way to the front of the VIP line? Sure, but I refuse to do it, since I have to pay $35 just to get into the damn place when I couldn't care less about the nightclub.

When you toke a doorman to get to the head of the line, it's called "line sliding." Some doormen go "line fishing" for people who will pay them to cut in front of others. In his most rapacious mode, a line-fisher will charge you to get to the front of the line, but you still won't be able to get in until you pay a second doorman at the entrance, after which you can finally pay the club cashier the cover charge to get in. I'm not opposed to line-sliding. I do it sometimes. And I'm not opposed to doormen getting toked for special treatment. These guys aren't paid a high wage by the clubs and must get tips to survive. But you should know that at the most popular clubs, one toke may not get you in—just closer to the entrance.

Snyder Says:
Love the Dolls.
Hate the nightclub.

Anyway, the doors open at 10:30. If you get into the general-public line at 10, you can expect to get into Pure by about 11.

Another problem for anyone who's there primarily for the Pussycat Dolls is that there's too much time between the performances, during which the club's house and hip-hop music is way too loud and there's no place to sit down unless you reserve a seat for bottle service. You can go out into Caesars and gamble, eat, or whatever (you get a hand-stamp when you enter Pure, so you can get back in), but the doormen at Pure didn't have any idea of the Pussycat Dolls show schedule and weren't even sure there were preset show times.

If you want to see what the Dolls look like without paying the cover charge, a Pussycat Dolls gambling pit right outside the nightclub opens about 9 p.m. every night. The dealers in this pit, which has 10 blackjack tables and two roulette tables, wear Pussycat Doll lingerie outfits, as do two dancers in cages at each end of the pit. The Dolls in the theater never get down to much less coverage than these dancers wear. Of course, the cage dancing out in the gambling pit isn't of the same caliber that you'll see in the lounge. (Videos of the Dolls on screens behind the pit might give you a better idea of the show.)

My recommendation? Go see the show if you also want to go to the nightclub. Pure is considered one of Vegas' better high-end, high-tech, hip nightclubs and it always has top DJs and a big crowd into the pick-up scene. If you don't care for nightclubbing, you can pass on this show.

SHADOW BAR
Caesars Palace
3570 S. Las Vegas Blvd., Las Vegas

Phone: (702) 731-7873
Hours: Dancers start at 9 p.m.
Minimum Age: 21
Cover Charge: None
Table Reservations: N/A
Full Bar: Yes
Food: No
Dress Code: No
Website: caesarspalace.com

The shadow dancers come on every night at 9 p.m. These are real live dancers behind translucent screens, backlit so that all you can see are their silhouettes. The best seats for watching the dancers are the barstools, so if one's available, belly up and enjoy the free show.

The shadow dancers are sexier than many of the dancers in the topless clubs and I've been trying to figure that out. One reason may be that they're actually good dancers. Also, it's mesmerizing to see just their silhouettes, because you can almost see skin, but not quite. Some dance topless behind the screen—or it certainly appears that they are and one of the bartenders told me they were. And they really work hard back there. I've never timed them, but I'm sure they dance for a half-hour or more before being relieved of shadow duty.

The Shadow Bar isn't a nightclub; it's just a bar. But as bars go, it's different and it deserves mention. There's no cover charge and a domestic beer costs $7. The music isn't too loud and it's a nice mix of modern and classic rock and top 40. Drinks are served up by flair bartenders who entertain by juggling the bottles. They're fun to watch and sometimes they compete with each other, and then pass out free drinks. Really.

Snyder Says:
Just sit right down and enjoy the free show.

STONEY'S ROCKIN' COUNTRY BAR
9151 S. Las Vegas Blvd. #300, Las Vegas

Phone: (702) 435-2855
Hours: Thurs.–Sun. 7 p.m.–4 a.m.
Minimum Age: 21
Cover Charge: $10; locals, $5
Table Reservations: N/A
Full Bar: Yes
Food: Yes; a few snack items
Dress Code: No; jeans and a T-shirt fit in just fine
Website: stoneysrockincountry.com

Stoney's Rockin' Country Bar is 25,000 square feet, the biggest one-level nightclub in the state. How big is 25,000 square feet? Think of a football field. If you stand at one corner of the playing field and cut it in half at the 50-yard line, that's 24,000 square feet. The main show-room at Sapphire, the "world's largest gentlemen's club," is 10,000 square feet.

Stoney's is run by the guy who used to manage Gilley's, the country-western bar at the now-gone New Frontier on the Strip. It has wait-resses in black satin bikini outfits with leather chaps who sometimes ride the mechanical bull on weekends. Since the place opened (shortly after the New Frontier closed), Stoney's has been experimenting with wet T-shirt contests, bikini bull-riding contests, mud-wrestling competitions, and all kinds of drink specials.

In the year that Stoney's has been in operation, it's continually altered its event calendar. I suspect at some point the club will settle down, but the experimentation makes my job difficult. I'd advise you to check Stoney's website for details, but the website is often wrong and I've even gotten wrong information calling the club.

At the time of this writing, the current calendar of events on Stoney's website says that Thursday is Ladies Night, with all ladies' drinks just $1 each. But I was in the club recently and the video screens around the room advertised both Thursdays and Sundays as Ladies Nights. Also, the website advertised Wednesday nights as mud-wrestling night, where for $20 customers can drink all they want (wine, well, and draft), and says Thursday through Sunday is $20 all-you-can-drink draft. But inside the club, the video screens advertised Friday and Saturday nights only as $20 all-you-can-drink nights, with no mention of Wednesday or Thursday.

Snyder Says:
A great shit-kickin' honky-tonk bar.

Also, the website said that Thursday, Friday, and Saturday nights host bikini bull-riding contests, with $500 in prize money. But on the Friday night I went to Stoney's, the contest was cancelled. The DJ said they "might" start the contests up again "next month." For quite a few months, Stoney's was advertising bikini bull riding on these nights, but there was no contest—just the bikini-clad waitresses riding the bull sporadically through the night.

Also, on Sunday nights, Stoney's used to have a wet T-shirt contest. Now they no longer have it.

Because all of these schedule and policy changes have occurred over a period of just a few months, with the website and telephone information not always in agreement with what I found in the club itself, I review the events with a warning that you may find something different from what I report. I'll try to keep my own website updated on what's happening there by checking it out regularly. I hope it settles down to a regular schedule. The bikini bull-riding contest and the mud-wrestling competition were both very popular at Gilley's. In fact, the bikini bull-riding contest was the only reason I ever went there.

Nightclubs Reviewed

Like Gilley's, Stoney's is a rowdy place where beer in longneck bottles is the drink of choice, cowboy hats and western shirts define the dress code, the crowd knows the words to every Travis Tritt ballad that blasts from the billion-decibel sound system, and they all sing along. Those who aren't line-dancin' out on the main floor can either watch the National Finals Rodeo on the two big-screen TVs or take their turns trying to ride the mechanical bull. With two full bars and numerous waitresses manning big tubs of bottled beer located everywhere, you never have to go far to pick up another cold one. There are also four pool tables, four lanes of machine bowling, a handful of video games, and a couple of electronic dart boards. This is not a sit-down crowd, so even when the joint is packed, you can usually find a seat at one of the comfortable booths or along the rails around the dance floor or the bull-riding arena.

A Primer on Line Dancing

The dance floor is huge. At line-dancing time, it's mostly women out there. I was born and raised in Detroit, so I know as much about line dancing as I do about steer roping. But I went to Stoney's a half-dozen times to try and figure it out. For those of you who are city boys like me, allow me to explain. Line dances have names like the "Swamp Thing," the "Sleazy Slide," "Black Velvet," the "Rio," the "Cha-Cha Slide," etc. If you're on the dance floor, you're supposed to know the steps. Thursday through Sunday at 7:30 p.m., Stoney's offers line-dancing lessons (or at least, that's what the website says).

Out of 100 people line-dancing, 94 of them will be women. Apparently, most guys are just not into line dancing, so don't feel like you have to learn it. Of the six guys out there, four of them have two left feet and keep shuffling left when all the ladies are shuffling right. Or maybe they're drunk. The other two guys are decked out in the fanciest cowboy duds you ever saw—two-toned boots with scrolled leatherwork, tight jeans with a big-ass brass buckle, western shirt with metallic silver piping, cowboy hat, the works. And these two guys have every dance step down to perfection. Maybe they teach line dancing or something. Is there such a thing as a professional line dancer?

How to Be a VIP

Thursday (and maybe Sunday) is Ladies Night at Stoney's, which means that all ladies get all drinks all night long for $1 each. Needless to say, this place is hoppin' with rowdy hard-drinking cowgirls on Thursday nights. In fact, it's hard to get in the door. I arrived at about 11 p.m. one Thursday night to find two lines to get in, one with 150 people stretching halfway down the mall where the club is located. The shorter line had maybe 10 people in it, but neither line was moving. I asked a guy wearing spiffy cowboy duds—ten-gallon hat and mother-of-pearl buttons on his shirt—standing in the short line about the difference between the two lines. "This one's for VIPs on the guest list," he said. I've been in Vegas long enough to know what a VIP is, so I walked up to the doorman with a ten-spot in my hand and asked if I could go in. "That won't do it tonight," he said. I added another ten and pushed the $20 toward him. "Go right in, sir," he said. VIP my ass. Very Impressive Payola.

Is ladies night a good bet for hooking up? Well, the ratio of women to men is definitely in your favor. And all that cheap booze for the ladies can't hurt either. But keep in mind that this crowd is mostly locals, not tourists, and girls who live here are probably not as loose as tourists who know that what happens in Vegas doesn't follow them home to Minnesota (providing they take certain precautions). But like I say, this book isn't a guide to picking up girls. We're looking for entertainment.

So if you're not into country music and you're not trying to pick up a girl, is it worth going to Stoney's for the show?

Hmmmmm …

Bikini Bull-Riding

As for the bikini bull-riding, if it's just the waitresses riding the bull every once in a while to entertain the crowd, it's not the caliber of show Gilley's used to have, where local strippers tried to undress while riding the bull. That was a blast. Now, the waitresses are adorable in their bikini-with-chaps ensembles, but it's not nearly as erotic as watching girls undress—even if they're just getting down to little bras and thongs—and it just doesn't have the same fun factor as the Gilley's-style show, where dudes from the audience were chosen to be judges and the girls on the bulls were trying to be as sexy as possible to win cash.

It's true that some of the women in the crowd try to ride the bull as they get drunker. And some are wearing little denim skirts, so when they go flying off the bull—it's inevitable—you get to see their panties, and that's actually sexier than watching the Stoney's waitresses. And occasionally, a girl from the crowd who rides the bull actually picks up her shirt and flashes her titties, just for the hell of it. Like I say, this is a rowdy drinking crowd and everybody's having a good time. But Stoney's has been advertising the old Gilley's-style contest off and on, so even though I've yet to see it happen at Stoney's, here's my review of the bikini bull-riding at Gilley's.

You couldn't miss the bull. He was right out in the center of a big arena at the far end of the main bar, nonchalantly tossing drunks off his back onto the padded floor. That had to hurt. When the DJ announced that the contest was starting, with $500

Nightclubs Reviewed

in prize money, you probably wondered how on Earth a girl in a bikini could ever maintain her dignity on that godforsaken contraption that kept making flying fools out of the brave souls who decided in their drunken stupor to entertain their friends by nearly breaking their necks. But this contest wasn't about dignity. It was about $500 bucks, pure and simple.

If you're a rodeo fan, you know that bull-riding is all about staying on that royally pissed-off creature from hell for eight seconds. That's all. Eight seconds. If you can last that long, you get scored based on your ability to stand up and smile after getting thrown and trampled, while the beast goes apeshit goring the rodeo clowns (who must be even crazier than the bull-riders, because there's no way they're getting paid enough to justify their job hazards).

Bikini bull-riding, on the other hand, isn't a duration event. You had that figured out about the time the MC started passing out score cards to a few lucky fans on the rail selected to be judges. These were big cards with numbers from 1 to 10 that the judges got to hold up after each girl's performance, just like they do in the Olympics for gymnastics and figure skating.

The half-dozen or so contestants each got about three minutes on the bull to show her stuff. The guy on the controls kept it nice and slow. No bucking, no wild spins. That mechanical beast just rocked nice and easy, with no intention of throwing any of these girls off his back. Each girl started out dressed—maybe in a little mini-dress or some tight cut-off shorts and a halter top—and she spent the first minute or so removing her clothes, down to her string-bra and micro g-string, all while riding the bull (and with you wondering how the hell she was going to get those shorts off). When she started doing splits and acrobatics, you realized that this was probably not just some drunk girl taking a dare from her friends. This was definitely a dancer, and there wasn't a cowboy in this place who could imagine doing what any of these girls were doing on that mechanical monster, no matter how slowly it was rocking. (And, frankly, you didn't want to see any of them try.)

On some nights, an amateur girl showed up to compete, who actually thought it was about staying on the bull. She might have, in fact, been pretty good at riding the bull, and she was probably with a proud boyfriend who told her she looks great in a bikini and could win that prize money. So she came out in her bra and bikini panties, mounted the bull, and sat there waiting for the guy at the controls to crank up the juice.

Which never happened.

And sometimes you had a dancer—and you knew she was a dancer because she had the costume and the boob job—who simply could not do her moves on that bull. Every time she tried to go into her routine, she flew off, legs akimbo.

The whole show lasted less than half an hour, so if you were in the mood for a long night of watching strippers strip, this probably wasn't your best choice. But this was a sexy show, and I always found that the judges—amateurs though they were, and drunken amateurs at that—generally did award the prize money to the girls who deserved it. I'd start going to rodeos if they added this event to the NFR.

The Wet T-Shirt Contest

As for the wet T-shirt contest on Sunday night—which has been canceled, but may return at some point—it's less than inspired. The night I saw it—it happens around 11:30 p.m.—the seven contestants were all amateurs. You can tell they're not pros: They're not wearing platform heels, they've got normal bikini panties on instead of stripper thongs, and they don't know how to dance, or even walk, like a stripper. That's fine with me, because I think amateur contests are way more fun than contests where pros compete. And all these girls were pretty cute in their underwear.

Each girl in the contest is called out on stage one at a time and she stands in a big washtub while she has a pitcher of water poured over her top. But Stoney's makes one big blunder—they supply all the girls with Stoney's T-shirts, or I assume they do, as every contestant was wearing a brightly-colored T-shirt with the Stoney's logo across the chest. Sorry, but that ain't how a wet T-shirt contest works. The whole point is that the girls wear the thinnest white cotton T-shirts they can find, usually cut off short and often sleeveless, and when the water hits the cloth, you can see nipples. It's almost like topless. And when they dance after they get wet, that little wet scrap of a T-shirt doesn't provide the kind of full coverage that T-shirts normally do.

Mud Wrestling on Wednesday

The mud-wrestling show allegedly starts sometime between 11 p.m. and midnight. This is another show they've been advertising, but I've never seen it happen. I saw it numerous times at Gilley's, and I'll assume Stoney's version will be the same. Lately, however, Stoney's hasn't even been open on Wednesday nights, despite what the website says.

At Gilley's, a couple of good-looking girls came out in bikinis and did three-minute matches until one girl managed to pin the other for a count of three. Then the winner got a break before she had to fight the next contender. They really did wrestle and they really were struggling to win. It was definitely not choreographed, so it was a hell of a lot more real than the WWE.

But I just don't get mud wrestling. The girls look great in their bikinis until they hit the mud. And unfortunately, they hit the mud as soon as they get out there. Then they just look like a couple of swamp things.

Are there guys who find this sexy?

I've seen some really hot oil-wrestling, jell-o-wrestling, and whipped-cream-wrestling shows in various parts of the country. The Hollywood Bowl in Hollywood used to do a fantastic oil-wrestling show. When you watch two girls oil wrestling in bikinis, it's a turn-on. You could fantasize jumping onto the mat with both of them right then and there. (In fact, they used to auction off the right to wrestle with one of the girls to the highest bidder, and some guys paid more than $100 for three minutes in the ring.) But mud wrestling? You're looking at a couple of sludge creatures that you really don't want anywhere near you.

Now, if they hosed the girls off between rounds or something ... I'd get a front-row seat every show. And if they auctioned off the hosing detail, they'd really rake in some bucks. But they just wrap these muddy girls up in towels when the match is done and scoot 'em out the back door.

Go figure.

So I'm of the opinion that Stoney's is a great shit-kickin' honky-tonk bar that may appeal to any guy who's trying to pick up a cowgirl on a Thursday night. And if the club is actually having a Gilley's-style bikini bull-riding contest on the weekends, with the local strippers competing, that show's easily worth the $5 cover, assuming you like country music and crowded honky-tonks. But if you're just in the mood for erotic entertainment, stick to the strip clubs.

13

Overview of the Shows

Ever since the "family-entertainment" scare of the 1990s, when casinos canned their topless shows in favor of amusements for the Baby Boomers' kiddies, the casinos have been losing show revenue to the strip clubs. Now, the casinos are fighting to get this money back. To keep their customers on property, they're offering a new assortment of topless revues, advertised as delivering some pretty steamy entertainment.

A number of shows in Las Vegas are billed as "adults only," but these are comedy performances. I'm assuming that anyone reading this book is primarily interested in erotic, more specifically strip-club-type, entertainment. So, I don't review Kevin Burke's one-man-show, *Defending the Caveman* at Excalibur, or *Lucky Cheng's Drag Cabaret*, or *Dirty Hypnosis Unleashed*, or any of the other adult-entertainment options this town has to offer that probably won't be around for long (in fact, Lucky Cheng's has just closed) and wouldn't fill the bill for a guy seeking something along the lines of a strip club anyway. If a show has no dancers taking their clothes off, or at least flashing their titties, it's not reviewed herein.

My show reviews are different from the reviews you might read online or in newspapers or magazines that cover Las Vegas entertainment. Most of those are written for the general public—a broad spectrum of men and women whose interests include a variety of entertainment options. I'm not writing for the general public. I'm assuming that anyone looking for a show using this guidebook is a guy with a one-track mind.

For example, I review both *Jubilee!* at Bally's and *X Burlesque* at the Flamingo, because both feature topless dancers. *Jubilee!* has a cast of 100 dancers and some of the most astonishing special effects you'll ever see in a stage production. If I were rating shows on production values, *X Burlesque* wouldn't even be in the same league. But in my rating system, special effects don't count. Half the dancers in *Jubilee!* are male, while the six female dancers who comprise the entire cast of *X Burlesque* are so much sexier and spend so much more time on stage than the 50 *Jubilee!* showgirls that *X Burlesque* beats *Jubilee!* hands down for any guy looking for something resembling a strip-club experience in a casino showroom.

Let me explain what I mean by "something resembling a strip-club experience in a casino showroom." If you're a tourist looking for a more risqué Vegas show where you get to see some beautiful nearly naked dancers, you'll enjoy a show like *X Burlesque*. But if you're a guy who likes watching strippers and you think *X Burlesque* might provide an actual strip-club experience, you'll likely be disappointed, even though *X Burlesque* is one of the sexier casino shows in town.

Watching a stripper is one thing: A striptease is personal and a stripper plays with and reacts to the crowd. Watching a dancer in a casino show imitate a stripper is something else again. A striptease-like dance number is impersonal. A dancer in a casino show just goes through her choreographed routine.

In the late 1980s, Tina Turner recorded a very popular hit song called "Private Dancer," allegedly the lament of a woman who worked as a stripper. The lyrics described the stripper's feelings while dancing and included lines like, "You don't look at their faces" and "You never ask them their names" and "You keep your eyes on the wall."

That song could never have been written by someone who had actually stripped for a living, or even spent much time watching strippers. The whole art of stripping is about eye contact with the audience. Show me a stripper who never looks at the faces of the men in the audience and I'll show you a stripper who will never make a buck in the business, no matter how good-looking she is. A stripper makes individual guys watching her feel like she's dancing for them, and she does it with her eyes. If you watch the same stripper on 10 different occasions, her routine will be different every time. It all depends on which guys she picks out to tease and how she proceeds based on each guy's responses to her. There's always a playfulness and spontaneity to stripping and the stripper's creativity and improvisations make her exciting to watch. A stripper on stage is always living in the moment and you never know what she's going to do next. The best strippers have fun on stage and you can't fake having fun.

I had a great seat for *X Burlesque*, right on the center aisle, literally three feet from the mini-stage. During the course of the show, every dancer had a turn or two on that stage, but not once did one of them look at me. They all "kept their eyes on the wall." There isn't a single improvised moment in the show and the overall effect is rehearsed rather than spontaneous, because it's not the bare boobs that make a stripper exciting so much as the lively, intelligent, teasing woman behind them. So if it's strippers you want to watch, casino shows will never satisfy you. No matter what a critic may say in a review about a casino show, no matter how much he raves about how "erotic" or "seductive" or "over the top" he found it, trust me, in most cases he's just trying to maintain the ad revenue stream for whatever publication he works for. No one with any concept of what goes on in the strip clubs would ever view casino production shows as highly erotic.

The dancers in casino shows can dance—in most cases a hell of a lot better than most strippers—but when it comes to pole and floor work and the real nitty-gritty stripper moves that make the boys go nuts with lust, the casino showgirls could all take lessons from the 18-year-olds over at Little Darlings.

You could take your wife or girlfriend to any casino show I review without making her feel uncomfortable, even though they feature topless dancers. (I'm assuming your wife or girlfriend isn't a total prude.) So if you're in Vegas with your significant other and you can't get away to a real strip club, these shows might be your next best bet. In fact, a few of the hotter shows are so good that I recommend them to any strip club devotee, as a different kind of sexy entertainment.

All the casino shows I review here have a minimum-age requirement of 18 years.

As I assume you're primarily looking for a show that will turn you on, I rate casino shows according to the same SPW scale I use to rate strip clubs, with 100% being the most arousing and 0% being about as sexy as a Daffy Duck cartoon. Here's a quick rundown of the ratings from top to bottom on the SPW Scale:

SPW: Statistical Probability of Wood

Show	Casino	SPW Rating
1. *Crazy Horse Paris*	MGM Grand	50%
2. *Sin City Bad Girls*	Las Vegas Hilton	47.5%
3. *Zumanity*	New York-New York	45%
4. *Crazy Girls*	Riviera	40%
5. *X Burlesque*	Flamingo	35%
6. *Bite*	Stratosphere	30%
7. *Peepshow*	Planet Hollywood	25%
8. *Fantasy*	Luxor	15%
9. Sin City Comedy	Planety Hollywood	10%
10. *Jubilee!*	Bally's	2%

Las Vegas casino shows are generally expensive, with ticket prices ranging from $35 to $100+. Locals are occasionally given a price break, so it's always smart to ask at the box office just in case. Guests of the hotel-casino are also sometimes given a special rate. Be sure to check in-room extras, or even look for packages that include show tickets when you're searching out a hotel in the first place. A lot of casino showrooms make half-price same-day tickets available at discount ticket outlets located throughout the city. (See below for information on these.) Also, casino shows are sometimes promoted through discount coupons distributed through local motels, rental-car offices, visitor centers, or in the freebie visitor magazines, and even if you don't have a coupon, the box-office cashier may be able to supply you with one. A good thing to remember in Vegas is that there's often a discount available on anything the casinos have to offer, so always ask. And, of course, this will be an area we pay close attention to at SinCity Advisor.com.

One way to get into a show free is to gamble in the casino. Showroom comps are among the easier freebies for gamblers at the table games to obtain. Unfortunately, this usually requires bets of $25 or more, sometimes for a number of hours, and this could make the cost of the show far more expensive than just buying a ticket. If you do play table games at this level, or if you play high-end slots or video poker, you'll often find that you can get show tickets comped just for asking.

My general approach to tickets for casino shows with assigned seating is to buy the cheap seats, then tip the maitre d' or usher for a better seat. This usually works when the show isn't sold out. In my reviews of the shows, I tell you which shows are your best bet for this ploy.

Discount Ticket Outlets

Discount ticket outlets offer tickets for some shows at discounts up to 50% off. These tickets are sold for shows on the day of purchase only and cannot be purchased online or over the phone; you must go in person to one of the outlets and purchase tickets as available. Also, the discount ticket offices don't sell you an actual ticket to the show, but a voucher you can trade for a ticket at the showroom box office. So you still have to go to the box office to get your seat assignment and you have to hope that they still have good seats available when you get there.

Tix4Tonight offers same-day mostly half-price discount show tickets. They have five outlets in Las Vegas, four of which are on the Strip (Las Vegas Blvd.): one across from New York-New York near the giant Coke bottle, another in the Hawaiian Marketplace just south of the Harley Davidson Café, a third in front of Neiman Marcus in the Fashion Show Mall, and a fourth between the Wynn and the Riviera. They also have one downtown location on Fremont Street at the front of the Four Queens casino. In my experience, the downtown location is the least crowded, often with no line at all, while I've waited in line as long as 30 minutes at some of the Strip locations. You cannot phone Tix4Tonight for advance information on show availability—you must show up at one of their box offices to see what they have available. They start posting that day's available shows at 9:30 a.m. and their box offices open at 10 a.m. For the best selection, arrive before noon.

All Access Tickets is a relatively new discount ticket service similar to Tix4Tonight with mostly 50% off same-day show tickets. They also offer a few next-day show tickets. Their main box office is at Circus Circus and opens at 9 a.m. You can call them about ticket availability at (702) 360-1111 if you are asking about a specific show, but they will not provide a full list of available shows over the phone. Also, tickets cannot be reserved or purchased over the phone, but must be purchased in person at one of their box offices. Four other outlets open at 10 a.m.: on the Strip at the South Point casino, Tahiti Village, and in the Fashion Show Mall; and on Flamingo Road in the Tuscany casino. As with Tix4Tonight, arrive early for the best selection.

The show prices I quote in my reviews are the full prices you'd pay at the casino showroom box office, online at the casino's website, or over the phone. Show tickets can also be purchased through other outlets, though additional service charges may be added.

14

Casino Shows Reviewed

BITE

Stratosphere, Theater of the Stars

Reservations: (702) 380-7711; (800) 998-6937
Show Times: Fri.–Wed. 10:30 p.m., dark Thurs.
Minimum Age: 18
Ticket Price: $49.45
Seating: General admission
Beverage Service: Yes
Website: stratospherehotel.com

SPW: 30%

The Lord Vampire is searching for his Queen of the Night. He sends his sexy minions, the Erotic Rock Angels—dancers with fangs—out into the showroom to pick women for him to consider. He chooses one pretty, but innocent-looking, member of the audience to be his queen. About the time he rips off her dress, you're pretty sure she must be part of the show, and when she loses her bra and starts dancing around in her panties, all doubts are gone. (I hope I'm not giving away too much of the plot here!) Anyway, this girl's astonishingly beautiful breasts would be a feast for any titman's eyes, so if that's what you came to this show for, you'll be happy.

The music is great—mostly classic hard rock from the '60s, '70s, and '80s. This happens to be the music that most strippers use in the clubs and it fits the sexy rebellious style of the *Bite* dancers very well. There must be two dozen classic tunes in the hour-plus show and you'll recognize all of them. You can get a pretty good overall feeling for the show just by looking at a list of some of the songs you'll hear.

From the 1960s: "Satisfaction" by the Rolling Stones; "Heartbreaker" by Led Zeppelin; and "Born to Be Wild" by Steppenwolf.

From the 1970s: "Cat Scratch Fever" by Ted Nugent; "Cold as Ice" and "Hot-Blood-

Snyder Says:
"Tits with teeth!"

ed" by Foreigner; "Welcome to My Nightmare" by Alice Cooper; "Witchy Woman" by the Eagles; and "Love Hurts" by Nazareth.

From the 1980s: "You Gotta Fight for the Right to Party" by the Beastie Boys; "Welcome to the Jungle" by Guns and Roses; and "You Shook Me All Night Long" by AC/DC.

Add a dozen more well-known hard-rock classics by Def Leppard, Heart, Ozzy Osborne, Twisted Sister, etc., plus the aria from the 1892 Italian opera *Pagliacci* (how'd that get in there?), and you get the picture.

The Strat's Theater of the Stars seats about 600, with table seating on three levels—a terrible theater for this type of show. It's simply too big. You want to focus on individual performers (primarily nearly naked dancers), best done at close range. So if you do go to see this show, be sure to tip the usher five bucks to get a good seat down in front. The theater attempts to compensate for its size by having two large video screens on either side of the stage, with a videographer who zooms in on individual performers throughout the show, but who wants to go to a theater to watch dancers on a video monitor?

Another reason to sit up close is that the choreographed production numbers leave a lot to be desired. The dancers' synchronization is slipshod at best. When they're supposed to be dancing in sync, they seem to compete with each other to stand out and capture the attention of the audience.

Most of the dancing is topless and each dancer gets a turn or two at a solo number. All eight of the girls have knockout-gorgeous dancers' bodies and every one of them can dance. Each has her own style, energy, and personality.

There's not much silicone in sight, so if your idea of a good topless show is a lot of bouncing big titties, you'll be pretty bored until the Lord Vampire picks his Queen. But as dancers, the Erotic Rock Angels are far more talented than any you'll see on stage in the local topless clubs, where silicone rules and dancing talent is scarce.

Some fairly mundane and unimpressive (for Vegas) magic is thrown into the show, as well as a couple of kinky and talented S&M aerialists. There's also a male singer who has a great voice. When he launched into Van Morrison's "Moondance" from the wings, I actually thought we were listening to the original recording, until he came out onto the stage singing.

If you want a drink during the show, my advice is to pick it up at the bar located right outside the showroom entrance before you go in. Cocktail service in the theater is slow.

CRAZY GIRLS
Riviera, Mardi Gras Pavilion

Reservations: (702) 794-9433; (877) 892-7469
Show Times: Wed.–Mon. 9:30 p.m., dark Tues.
Minimum Age: 18
Ticket Price: $50.45/$72.50
Seating: Maître D'
Beverage Service: No
Website: rivierahotel.com

SPW: 40%

Crazy Girls opened at the Riviera in 1988. Not many Vegas production shows have been running uninterrupted for more than 20 years, so they must be doing something right.

One of the things they definitely did right was install that bronze relief of the *Crazy Girls* dancers at the front of the casino on the Strip. To celebrate the show's 10th anniversary in 1998, the Riv commissioned Santa Fe sculptor Michael Conine to create a life-size rearview bronze sculpture of the seven dancers standing in a row, arms around each others' waists, wearing only their thongs. When the Riv unveiled the artwork, the National Organization for Women launched a formal protest, claiming the sculpture degraded women, reducing them to nothing but bronze pieces of ass (literally!). A Nevada congressman even tried to get the state legislature to ban the sculpture from public display as indecent. Las Vegans, however, loved it (is this a great town or what?) and newspapers all over the world carried photos and stories about it. Today, the brassy bottoms of the sculpture continue to be rubbed daily by tourists, who often pose for photos with the artwork. The sculpture is widely considered a Las Vegas landmark, right up there with the Mirage volcano, the Treasure Island pirate ship, and the Fremont Street Experience.

Crazy Girls was one of the first Vegas shows to emphasize topless dancers, minimize the variety acts, and completely do away with big production numbers. But when I saw the show about three years ago,

I thought it was on its last legs. The dance routines struck me as tired and unimpressive. Most of the numbers, including the few solos, were performed with lip-synching. And the juggler was underwhelming.

The Revamped Show is Hot!

I'm happy to report that all this is no longer a problem. I saw a totally revamped show on my most recent visit, with some really hot dancers who get down to the tiniest g-strings you'll ever see (you almost don't see them). All seven dancers are in great shape, very talented, and bursting with personality. If you're a tit man, there's not much silicone in this group. (Only one dancer has an obvious boob job.) Most of the girls are small-breasted, but still lovely to look at.

Snyder Says: The tiniest g-strings you'll ever see ...

I knew this show had gone through some big changes right from the opening number, when seven dancers in little black dresses come into the theater aisles dancing to Motley Crue's hard-rockin' "Girls, Girls, Girls" and lose their dresses on stage at the end of the song. Quite a few rock numbers in the show now include Aerosmith's "Pink," which involves four dancers doing a striptease on a revolving pink bed with dynamite floor work—or in this case, mattress work—with more leg spreads in their little pink thongs than you'd ever expect to see in a casino show.

The lip-synching has been reduced to a few classic show tunes that work. "Whatever Lola Wants (Lola Gets)," from the musical

Damn Yankees, is performed by a solo dancer who starts out dressed in a skimpy schoolgirl outfit and gets down to her g-string while writhing around on a giant stuffed phallus. The whole group dances and strips to Ruth Wallis' hilarious "You Gotta Have Boobs," from her off-Broadway hit, *Boobs: The Musical*. The only other lip-synched song was "How Could You Believe Me When I Said I Loved You, When You Know I've Been a Liar All My Life?," a song from the 1951 Fred Astaire/Jane Powell movie, *Royal Wedding*, though this recording of the song is sung cabaret-style by Eartha Kitt.

The show lasts about 70 minutes and it moves fast. In addition to the seven dancers, comic/magician Tony Douglas does a couple of short sets of fairly decent parlor magic. He's a funny guy, though personally I don't think the show needs him. Why interrupt first-class dancers with a second-rate comedy/magic act? And believe me, the dancers are first-rate. Beautiful. Sexy. Having fun.

MGM GRAND'S CRAZY HORSE PARIS
MGM Grand, Crazy Horse Paris Cabaret

Reservations (702) 891-7777; (866) 740-7711
Show Times: Wed.–Mon. 8 p.m. and 10:30 p.m., dark Tues.
Minimum Age: 18
Ticket Price: $50.50/$60.50
Seating: Assigned seating
Beverage Service: Yes
Website: mgmgrand.com

SPW: 50%

Crazy Horse Paris is one of the sexiest shows you'll ever see in a casino showroom. I can't imagine any guy who likes watching strippers not liking this show. These dancers are just too gorgeous.

I first saw this show some years ago when it was called *La Femme*, and at that time it was uninspired. A dozen beautiful young women, every one with a body to die for, all appeared to be not only ballet-trained dancers, but athletes and gymnasts as well. And throughout the hour-long show, these truly fine specimens of nubile perfection often wore little more than the tiniest black triangles of cloth. Still, the show itself wasn't sexy. The problem was that the dancers were never central to the show, but more like a canvas for the lighting technician to paint pretty patterns on. I suspect the director was some theatrical design major whose definition of a sexy girl is one whose pumps match her handbag. This was a show you could bring your grandparents to and Grandma wouldn't even make Gramps cover his eyes.

So I wasn't thrilled at the prospect of seeing the show again, as I assumed the new version, whether called *La Femme* or *Crazy Horse Paris*, would just be more artsy-fartsy lighting effects. Wrong. All 12 dancers in the current version are something special. The lighting effects have been toned down considerably, so you really get to see those beautiful bodies. And you'll definitely fall under their spell.

Legs, Legs, Legs …

In addition, the music is consistently well-chosen for the dance numbers. There's Rod Stewart's classic 70s hard-rock hit, "Hot Legs," popular with strippers everywhere for decades. Five dancers lie in a row on their backs with their legs in the air, asses stage front, and the dancing comes close to stripper floor work. Then there's the old jazz instrumental standard "Wabash Blues," to which a single dancer, visible only from the waist down, spends the whole song just touching and caressing her legs— one of which is bare, the other clad in a thigh-high black-silk stocking. She finishes by slowly removing her thong panties. The light goes out and you start breathing again. The whole show is like this—delivering one fetish fantasy after another.

Snyder Says:
One fetish fantasy after another …

The show sports a lot of visual humor, some subtle and some not so subtle. And though again, I'm not one for lip-synching, the dancer who does Eartha Kitt's "My Champagne Taste (and Your Beer Bottle Pockets)" is a first-rate comedienne. A dancer performs a great strip-tease number wearing a six-inch crucifix; and another striptease takes place on a red-velvet couch that's shaped like a pair of full lips.

The show's obligatory variety acts are two groups called the Quid-dlers, and the Scott Brothers. It's hard to describe exactly what these guys do. The Quiddlers' act was a comical mixture of break-dancing and pantomime. The Scott Brothers' number was a truly bizarre rendition of Michael Jackson as a midget performing with a monkey. I won't even try to explain it any further, but they really cracked me up.

Tickets for *Crazy Horse Paris* cost either $50.50 or $60.50. Take my advice and spring for the $60 seats, as close to the dancers as you can get. If front-row seats are available, grab them. The room was allegedly designed to replicate the Crazy Horse Theatre in Paris. Bad decision. The customers seated at tables at the back of each of the three levels have a better view of the backs of heads than of the stage and dancers. Don't plan on getting a better seat by tipping the usher; the seats up front are too often sold out. Since the price difference between the worst seats and the best is only $10, don't take a chance on getting stuck with a bad seat.

Casino Shows Reviewed

FANTASY
Luxor, Atrium Showroom
Reservations: (702) 262-4000; (800) 557-7428
Show Times: Mon.–Sun. 10:30 p.m.
Minimum Age: 18
Ticket Price: $53/$58.50/$64/$68.40
Seating: Assigned seating
Beverage Service: Yes
Website: luxor.com

SPW: 15%

What bugs me most about this show is the bait-and-switch. The outdoor billboards, the ad posters inside Luxor, and the promotional videos all feature hot-looking babes in sexy lingerie. The show's slogan is "The Strip's Most Seductive Topless Show." When you get to the show, however, you discover it's really just a showcase for a singer and a comedian who don't appear in any of the ads! Honest advertising for this show would say: "Appearing tonight in the Atrium Showroom, singing sensation Stephanie Jordan and hilarious comedian-imperson-ator Sean Cooper!" But since Luxor knows no one's ever heard of Stephanie Jordan or Sean Cooper, the show is sold as a hot kinky top-less revue, which it most assuredly is not.

Stephanie Jordan has a powerful voice, but she's wasting her tal-ent here. The half-dozen or so songs she sings are unknown forgettable tunes written specifically for *Fantasy*. I'd love to hear her belt out a few classic torch songs or ballads, but alas. She's definitely the sexiest girl in this show and she never even loses her top.

Likewise Sean Cooper. He sings. He dances. He does comedy bits and impersonations of James Brown, Michael Jackson (in whiteface!), Sammy Davis, Jr., and Tina Turner (yes, he does Tina Turner!). His Sammy Davis impersonation is particularly appropriate, because Sam-my, like Sean, was a multi-talented singer, dancer, and comedian … just a weird little black-Jewish beatnik-hipster in a class by himself. Sean Cooper should get himself out of this show and onto a stage where

249

he can do an hour or so on his own and the audience is there to see him, not coming to see a topless show and wondering what the hell he's doing on the stage.

What's especially irritating is that the show seems to start out with promise. After Stephanie Jordan's opening song, three dancers frolic topless on a bed to the old Vanity 6 hit, "Nasty Girl." You may recall that Vanity 6 was the lingerie-clad girl group put together by Prince in the early 1980s. I always liked "Nasty Girl" and the bed scene in *Fantasy* is cute, like a Roger Vadim-inspired pajama party. There's a lot of business with leap frogging and pillow fighting and girl tumbling.

Stephanie Jordan and funnyman Sean Cooper steal the show.

Unfortunately, the only other memorable dance number is a classic striptease routine by a dancer named "Jen," performed to Christina Aguilera's "Nasty Naughty Boy," a pop

Snyder Says:
Great singer, funny comic, false advertising ...

One of the *Fantasy* girls.

song that has one of my all-time favorite lyrics: "I wanna give you a little taste of the sugar below my waist!"

All the other dancing in the show is standard, choreographed, showgirl stuff. None of the group dance numbers—or individual dancers—stand out, and even though the dancers are topless, none of the dancing is erotic. The *Fantasy* dancers are as beautiful and sexy as any I've ever seen, and I went to this show to see them show off. I felt robbed.

The Atrium Showroom is a classic theater with a proscenium stage and standard seating. It was designed for production shows, not intimacy, and *Fantasy* is ultimately a production show. No drinks are served inside the theater, but you may bring them from the bar right outside the theater, provided you put it into a plastic cup that you can get at the entrance.

Ticket prices range from $53 to $68, with the higher price for seats closer to the stage. All seats are assigned and a tip to the usher may not get you a better seat, because the show often sells out. But save your money and just get the cheap ticket; there's no reason to sit up front. Better yet, take your $60, head over to Spearmint Rhino, have yourself a couple of beers and a couple of lap dances, and go home happy.

JUBILEE!

Bally's, Jubilee Theater

Reservations: (702) 967-4567; (800) 237-SHOW
Show Times: Sat.–Thurs. 7:30 p.m. and 10:30 p.m., dark Fri.
Minimum Age: Topless 18; Covered 13
Ticket Price: $60.65/$80.65/$101.15
Seating: Assigned seating
Beverage Service: No
Website: harrahs.com

SPW: 2%

The *Jubilee!* showgirls don't really perform much as dancers. I'm sure most of them have had formal training and you can tell that they *could* dance. Every once in a while they kick their legs up and only dancers can kick like that. But mostly they just strut around and pose in moth-sized fake eyelashes, buckets of makeup, and headdresses almost as big as they are, with lots of feathers and sequins. The major element of suspense is watching to see if one of them tips over.

In addition to showgirls, *Jubilee!* features showboys—a few dozen male dancers wearing rhinestone-studded tuxedos or weird glittering costumes that would get them labeled as gay even on Halloween.

And forget about the showgirls' titties. Those tits come and go so fast, you'll hardly notice them. Just view this show for its extravaganza value. Samson tears down the temple walls after Delilah shears his locks. The *Titanic* sinks. You'll get to see a tribute to Fred Astaire and Ginger Rogers—the segment with the most dancing, but it's ballroom dancing in gowns, not pole dancing in thongs. And you'll get to see a great juggler, a superb aerialist, and an astonishing hand-balancing act.

Don't Look for a Theme

One thing you should definitely not expect is a unifying theme. There isn't one. The only thing Samson and Delilah have to do with the *Titanic,* and Fred and Ginger is the over-the-top costumes and special effects.

The show's program divides the production into seven acts. Don't try to make sense of it unless you've just finished chewing up a few peyote buttons. For example, Act Five is titled: "Titanic," which includes not only the flooding of the boiler room, but a lingerie fashion show. Now perhaps the *Titanic* had a lingerie fashion show. I can accept that as a possibility. But why, after the boat sinks to the strains of "Nearer My God to Thee," does the act end with dancers in electric-blue spandex leotards gyrating to the tune of "Yankee Doodle Dandy"? I had to double-check my program to see if a new act had begun or if this was still part of the sinking of the *Titanic.* Yep, the *Titanic* act ends with a full combat brigade of dancers marching in front of the billowing folds of Old Glory. My recollection of the *Titanic* disaster was that the British ship was heading for New York, but never got there. Did the U.S. Navy actually sink the *Titanic?* Like I say, don't try to figure it out.

I think you can tell a lot about a show just by looking at the musical script. None of this is stripper music. None of this is even music that was written in the last 50 years. Rock 'n' roll? Too modern. Plan on hearing lots of schmaltzy old classics like: "My Heart Belongs to Daddy," "There's No Business Like Show Business," "Pack Up Your Troubles in Your Old Kit Bag," "Puttin' on the Ritz," "Tea for Two," "Dancing Cheek to Cheek," "Let's Call the Whole Thing Off," "In the Still of the

Snyder Says:
A hundred nipples on the stage and not a woody in the house.

Night," "Begin the Beguine," "Smoke Gets in Your Eyes," "With a Song in My Heart," "A Pretty Girl is Like a Melody"... Enough said? Your grandparents will leave the theater with shining eyes and a jaunty spring in their step.

Jubilee! has been playing at Bally's for more than 25 years. The original producer was Donn Arden, a legendary Vegas showman who hit the scene in 1958 with his racy (at the time) topless review, *Lido de Paris*, at the now-demolished Stardust Casino. *Jubilee!* is Arden's ultimate Las Vegas production show. There's a cast of at least 100 performers, half of them showgirls who perform topless on and off throughout the extravaganza, so if you've never seen a classic Vegas show and you have any interest whatsoever in the history of Las Vegas entertainment and the types of shows that initially gave Vegas its "anything-goes" reputation, you must see *Jubilee!* This show is a true anachronism and if it ever dies, a part of Vegas will die with it. But if you go, my advice is to get one of the cheap seats. There's not much reason to be close to the stage for this type of production.

PEEPSHOW
Planet Hollywood, Chi Theater

Reservations: (702) 785-5000; (877) 333-9474
Show Times: Mon., Tues., Thurs., and Sun. 9 p.m., Fri. and Sat. 8 p.m. and 10:30 p.m., dark Wed.
Minimum Age: 18
Ticket Price: $84.80/$96.05/$126.20/$200.85
Seating: Assigned seating
Beverage Service: Yes
Website: lasvegaspeepshow.com

SPW: 25%

Three dancers strip out of their little plaid schoolgirl outfits and climb into a four-foot-tall glass vat of milk that's sitting on the stage in Wicked Wendy's Flyer, an oversized red wagon. Once submerged to their necks, they remove their bras, then pull down their panties, pressing their bodies up against the sides of the glass. (A giant red wagon? A 200-gallon vat of milk? Schoolgirls with their panties down? I'm sure there's some deep symbolism at work here.) Note that I said they *pull down* their panties, not they *take off* their panties. When they press up against the glass, you can see their panties are at mid-thigh level and they appear to be bare from the panties up. But because they're in milk, not water, you can't really see anything but milk in the cracks and crevices you're focused on. (Not that I was focused on the cracks and crevices. I was actually trying to figure out the symbolism, which is reminiscent of Ingmar Bergman's 1960 film classic, *The Virgin Spring*.) In any case, this has to be one of the sexiest effects I've ever seen in a casino show.

The musical accompaniment to this craziest of stripteases is Kelis' 2003 rap hit "Milkshake" ("My milkshake brings the boys to the yard!"), sung live by one of *Peepshow's* backup singers, who does a dynamite job with it. Believe me, this milkshake will bring the boys to Planet Hollywood!

None of the music is recorded. The lead singer, Shoshana Bean (note that this show's leads change often, and this review reflects the current players), is a former Broadway musical star. The live five-piece band, two female backup singers, and a couple of male singers are all talented.

The songs that accompany the dance numbers are inspired and you never know what to expect next. There's jazzman Jimmy Smith's "Stay Loose"; the Commodores' funk ode to big tits, "She's a Brick House"; Dionne Warwick's "You'll Never Get to Heaven"; and Nina Simone's classic, "It's a New Day" (sung by one of the male singers who belts it out with incredible passion). This song accompanies a striptease with the only top-of-the-line pole dancing I've ever seen in a casino show. The dancer who performs the lead in this number is breathtaking—legs to die for. Aerosmith's "Pink (Is the Color of Passion)" backs up a weird number where a member of the audience (allegedly) is tied to a bed in his boxer shorts, then teased by a bevy

Snyder Says:
This is the sexiest Vegas-style production show in town.

of dancers crawling all over him until he's finally painted pink and wheeled off with his hands cupped over the tits of the show's co-star, Holly Madison. Connie Francis's schmaltzy old "Teddy" (a love song to her childhood teddy bear) is used for a striptease on a bearskin rug. There's something almost sacrilegious about this. R&B singer Ginuwine's "Ride on My Pony" serenades a blindfolded striptease by a dancer who undresses while swinging overhead on a saddle. Metaphorically, the saddle makes sense, given the song's chorus: "If you're horny, let's do it! Ride it, my pony! My saddle's waitin! Come and jump on it!" But what's with the blindfold?

Anyway, the 14 dancers get topless in some numbers, though I don't understand why they wear pasties in others. I personally find pasties unattractive and I see no reason for them.

Holly Madison, the co-star of the show, is primarily known for having been Hugh Hefner's "#1 Girlfriend" on the fatuous "reality" TV show, "The Girls Next Door." This means that she slept in Hef's bedroom, while the lesser "girlfriends" on the show slept in their own rooms down the hall. Now there's a claim to fame: She got to sleep with an 80-year-old billionaire on TV. Prior to being "discovered" by Hef, she was a Hooters waitress. Madison has one of those classic stripper boob jobs that I find … frightening. It looks painful, like she had a couple of extra large cantaloupes implanted under her skin. You just know, when she lies down those titties keep pointing skyward. What on Earth was Hefner doing with this girl? He's older than I am, so he knows what real tits look like. (Granted, she does have a superb butt.) Anyway, she can't sing and she can't dance, but she's cute as a button and you get to see her nipples at the end.

The female dancers are often accompanied in the group numbers by a couple of talented male dancers/gymnasts/acrobats. These male dancers are, in fact, the most talented dancers in the show. Shoshana Bean has an adequate voice and a bubbly personality, but what's with the outfits they stick her in? The wardrobe director should be shot at dawn. Ms. Bean is just a bit too plump to be running around a stage in bedroom lingerie (either camp up her outfits to play the "hefty-mama-sex-queen" image or let her wear something a bit more staid).

The Chi Showroom, formerly the Theater for the Performing Arts, is a large classic theater with tiered seating (for 1,350) and a balcony. The stage has three runways that jut out into the audience, with table seating down front. The theater has beverage service and a domestic beer costs $8.

The show's title is taken from Holly Madison's character, "Little Bo Peep," an innocent young girl who knows nothing of the ways of the world. (I'm sure Hefner would say they're stretching it a tad.) The story line is that this young girl falls into a fantasy dream world (kind of like *Alice Through the Looking Glass*—except this looking glass happens to be a one-way peep-show mirror), where she's guided into erotic adventures by the "Peep Diva." In other words, there's no story line other than a flimsy excuse to get Holly's top off. At the end, as our former Prez would say, "Mission accomplished." In any case, this is a fun show and it's surprisingly sexy for such a big production. The dancers are all gorgeous and talented and spend a lot of time on stage stripping down to (then dancing in) g-strings, sometimes topless, and sometimes in pasties. But then, you never know what you'll see when you drop your quarter into the slot at a peep show.

SIN CITY BAD GIRLS
Las Vegas Hilton, Shimmer Cabaret Showroom

Reservation Phone: (800) 222-5361
Show Times: Mon.–Sat., 9 p.m.
Minimum Age: 18
Ticket Price: $45/$55
Seating: General admission
Beverage service: Yes
Website: lvhilton.com

SPW: 47.5%

First, one girl dances around in her plaid schoolgirl micro-skirt that doesn't quite hide her white cotton panties. Then a second schoolgirl comes out and they start climbing on the rope netting that runs up the walls on either side of the stage front. Just a couple of innocent young girls having fun on the playground. Nice view!

Then a third schoolgirl enters, followed by the stern schoolmarm, who looks all business in her horn-rimmed glasses and her straight knee-length skirt, as she slaps a wooden pointer menacingly into her hand. And while the first two schoolgirls start losing their clothes as they frolic, oblivious to the presence of their teacher, the third schoolgirl and the teacher start to take each other's clothes off. Ultimately, all three schoolgirls and the teacher wind up dancing around the playground topless in their panties. I'm sure this happens all the time in schoolyards these days.

But school's not over yet! No sooner have teacher and schoolgirls left the playground than two more schoolgirls enter the scene, already topless, and in their plaid mini-skirts they perform an aerial routine on a spinning hoop to the strains of "Sweet Child of Mine," a Guns N' Roses classic that's performed live by a rock trio (guitar, keyboards, and drums) who supply all the music for the show. And as soon as these girls are done playing on the hoop, the band launches into Jet's "Are You Gonna Be My Girl?" and more topless schoolgirls come out to play. Ah, recess. It was always my favorite subject.

But I get ahead of myself... The schoolgirl montage doesn't happen until well into the second half of this production. This show is so good, I hardly know where to start.

So, let's start with Lorena Peril, the singer who is the show's star. Wow, can this girl sing! She's so sexy and commands the stage so dynamically that even when the topless dancers are onstage, it's hard to take your eyes off her. In the opening number, an original song for this show—probably titled either "Sin City Bad Girls" or "Rock On, Top Off" (a repeating line from the chorus)—seven dancers strip out of skimpy denim jackets and skirts to dance topless in pink and black-patent-leather platform go-go boots and matching bikini bottoms.

But I can't stop watching Lorena! She's wearing a denim outfit similar to the ones the dancers came out in, but she also has a cut-off undershirt that she never removes. The shirt is chopped to a length that just manages to cover her otherwise bare breasts and as she dances, the shirt rises up to the point where you can almost—but not quite—catch a glimpse of her nipples. This may sound crazy, but with topless girls all over the stage, I can't stop trying

Snyder Says:
Lorena Peril is HOT! This show rocks!

to see the tits on the one girl who's not topless! Do I need a shrink or what? But I'm sure I wasn't the only guy watching that flimsy scrap of T-shirt; whole websites are devoted to this "tits from below" fetish. The opening number ends with a rocking version of the Cars' "Shake It Up!"

Lorena then sings a soulful rendition of the Police's "Roxanne (You Don't Have to Put on the Red Light)." This song accompanies a kind of ballet striptease in reverse. It starts with a solo dancer wearing nothing but a thong, who slowly dresses as more dancers enter the stage. The band then incongruously segues into Nickelback's raunchy "Something in Your Mouth." The lyrics to this song are … should I say "suggestive?" It's an ode to "the pretty little lady with the pretty pink thong" and "you look so much cuter with something in your mouth."

Then the band moves onto Lenny Kravitz's "American Woman," in which two dancers in cut-off denim shorts and gold bras do a pole dance. I think these dancers might be better pole dancers than this number shows, because they use a mobile pole that they push onto the stage for this one sequence. A stripper pole really should be firmly anchored at both the top and bottom to allow the dancers freedom to move without fear of tipping it over.

Lorena (who portrayed Christina Aguilera in the show *American Superstars)* then sings Christina's "You Nasty Boy," while dancers in flowing bedroom negligees circulate through the audience teasing whatever nasty boys they can find. Then there's a cover of Rihanna's "Bad

Girl (What a Bad Little Girl I Am!)"

Now we get to the cowgirl segment that starts when a stooge from the audience is brought on stage and tied up in a dorky cowboy suit, while five dancers in bikini cowgirl outfits tease him mercilessly to the band's rollicking rendition of Big and Rich's country-western hit, "Save a Horse, Ride a Cowboy." Then Lorena launches into Gretchen Wilson's hard-driving "All Jacked Up," while two cowgirls in little tutus dance around. (Cowgirls in tutus? "All jacked up" means drunk in this song, which is about getting wasted at a bar after work, so maybe cowgirls wear tutus when they're drunk. Whatever, it's cute …) Then the drummer gets to take his turn on a country-western number, singing Trace Adkins' "Honky Tonk Badonkadonk." This one is performed by four topless dancers in electric-blue satin corsets.

The three-piece band is superb. They move effortlessly from rock to country to blues to jazz to ballads. And although they perform one song after another that has been recorded by well-known groups, they never attempt to mimic the originals, but put their own stamp on every song. I should also mention that all the dancers are really talented and you definitely want to get a front row seat for this show, because it is hot Hot HOT, start to finish.

A few of the other memorable numbers are stripteases to Joe Cocker's "You Can Leave Your Hat On," a fan dance to Foreigner's "Hot Blooded," a couple of sexy nurses with stethoscopes who get topless to Robert Palmer's "Bad Case of Loving You," and a duet between Lorena and the guitar player, singing Rod Stewart's "Hot Legs," with three topless dancers providing the leg action.

I was surprised that Lorena tackled Bette Midler's "Long John Blues," what with Bette having her own showroom in Vegas now. Bette has such a powerful voice and so totally owns any song she adds to her repertoire that few singers would risk being compared to her. Lorena Peril did this wailing blues solo, with no dancers, spotlight on just her, and she nailed it in her own style. If you're not familiar with vintage Bette Midler, this song is from her 1977 *Live at Last* album and has some of the nuttiest (and dirtiest!) lyrics of any song Bette has ever sung, and she's done a lot of nutty dirty songs. Doctor Long John is a dentist and the lyrics include such lines as, "He took out his trusted drill and he told me to open wide, He said he wouldn't hurt me but he'd fill that hole inside," and, "You thrill me when you drill me," and … You get the picture.

For the grand finale, the band ripped into AC/DC's "You Shook Me All Night Long" and we get one last look at Lorena Peril and those seven gorgeous topless babes.

Tickets for this show are $45 for general admission or $55 for VIP seating. Spend the $55 for the seats up front. You won't regret it. The Shimmer Cabaret is a medium-size (340-seat) theater with a classic proscenium stage that has a short runway. Get a runway seat if you can. Locals can get a general ad-mission seat for $33. If you get a general ad-mission seat, get there early (8:30) to grab the closest seat to the stage that you can.

There is bev-erage service in the theater, but most of the service takes place be-fore the show starts. You can also stop at the bar in back of the theater and pick up a drink. A domestic beer is $5.50.

SIN CITY COMEDY

Planet Hollywood, Harmon Theater

Reservation Phone: (702) 836-0836
Show Times: 7 p.m., nightly
Minimum Age: 21
Ticket Price: $34/$50
Seating: General admission
Beverage service: Yes
Website: planethollywoodresort.com

SPW: 10%

The advertising for this hour-and-fifteen minute production says that the show "puts the sin back into Sin City," by bringing together some of the nation's top standup comics with burlesque dancers. The show opens with the "Sin City Dollz," a five-dancer troupe in leather trench coats, strutting and posing to Henry Mancini's theme from "Peter Gunn." They lose the coats and pick up feather boas to continue dancing in corsets and stockings to "You're the Boss" by the Brian Setzer Orchestra. They're all gorgeous dancers and I'm a hardcore Brian Setzer fan, but sad to say, they never take off any more of their outfits and you won't see topless girls in this show.

The highlight for anyone looking for sexy entertainment is the aerial routine performed by two dancers introduced as Erica and Fagan. Both have dynamite bodies and they do some breathtaking acrobatics hanging from ribbons of cloth. Their full-split positions in those little bikini outfits are highly erotic.

But this is essentially standup comedy with an opening dance number and a couple of sexy aerialists in between the comics' sets. Don't go to "Sin City Comedy" if you're more interested in seeing something sexy than funny.

I expect the two comics will change as time goes on. The night I went, Bill Tucker—a veteran Vegas showroom comic—was the opening act and Greg Vaccariello was the headliner. Tucker is one of those rubber-faced comics who gets some of his biggest laughs with his goofy expressions; his "Turkeyman" routine is priceless. Vaccariello is a New York comic who capitalizes on his Italian heritage and all the Italian stereotypes.

The Harmon Theater is a no-frills affair with chair seating on two levels. I don't know what you get with the expensive tickets, because I paid for a cheap seat and the usher told me just to "sit anywhere," so I grabbed a front-row seat and didn't even tip him. Free tickets for this show are often passed out on the Strip and two-for-one tickets may be available at the box office for locals. At present, they're just trying to get the seats filled, so you might find other deals online. There's a full bar at the back of the theater and you can bring a drink to your seat, but there are no tables in the theater. A domestic beer is $6.

Snyder says This is primarily a comedy show. Go for the laughs.

X BURLESQUE
Flamingo, Second City Theater
Reservations: (702) 733-3333; (800) 221-7299
Show Times: Mon.–Sun. 10 p.m.
Minimum Age: 18
Ticket Price: $49.95/$61.95
Seating: General admission
Beverage Service: Yes
Website: harrahs.com

SPW: 35%

X Burlesque is another show with no theme whatsoever, just one dance number after another with no attempt at any logical segues, which is fine with me. The numbers include a lot of classic striptease styles and props, from fans and feather boas to a scene with two girls in a bathtub.

The music is an eclectic mix, to say the least. One dance might be done to rock 'n' roll, the next to Dixieland jazz, and the one after that to a classical symphonic arrangement. The songs are all great for strippers to dance to. I don't care much for Christina Aguilera, but I do like her "Candyman," which is not the schmaltzy old Sammy Davis Jr. song, but a jazzy Pointers Sisters-type tune that's anything but schmaltzy. ("He's a one-stop, gotcha hot, makin' all the panties drop, sweet sugar candyman!") If you don't know this song, you can watch the music video of it on Youtube. You'll also hear "I Like the Way You Move" by the Australian group Body Rockers, "Cherry Pie" by Poison, and "When You Got It, Flaunt It," a really great show tune you might recall from *The Producers.* They even used the uncensored version of Buckcherry's "Crazy Bitch," a way-over-the-top hard-rock song you'll never hear on radio or TV, since the chorus begins with the words, "Hey, you're a crazy bitch! But you fuck so good I'm on top of it!"

This is not a variety show: no singers, jugglers, acrobats, ventriloquists, or magicians. The only break from the dancing is a 20-minute set by a stand-up comic. The night I saw the show, it was Nancy Ryan, who does put-down type humor in the Don Rickles vein. I liked her. Other local comics sometimes fill this spot.

Beautiful Bodies in Motion

So you've got six gorgeous, talented, top-less dancers with great bodies, a perfect small showroom, and fun music start to finish. Other than for the short set by the comic, the entire show is performed by the same six girls do-ing solo and group numbers. They work hard for their money and really work up a sweat. If you like watching beautiful bodies in motion, this show won't let you down.

Snyder Says: It's always a pleasure to watch beautiful bodies in motion.

There are two ticket prices for this show, though the seats aren't assigned. The extra $12 gets you "VIP seating," whatever that is. Don't pay for it. I got the general-admission ticket, gave the usher five bucks at the door, and got the best seat in the house.

The Second City Theater is essentially an intimate comedy club, so there really aren't any bad seats. The main stage is small and for this show they have another square mini-stage in the center of the room with a stripper pole. When you slip the usher $5, point to a seat on the center aisle, near the main stage front and right next to the mini-stage. You'll have a great close-up view of all those gorgeous danc-ers.

A beer will cost you $8 and they don't let you bring in a drink from outside. That's about the same price for a beer that you'll pay in many real strip clubs. The show is about an hour and a half long, so if you want to drink during the show, it'll cost you.

Seven gorgeous, talented, topless dancers with great bodies, a perfect small showroom, and fun music start to finish.

ZUMANITY
New York-New York, Zumanity Theatre
Reservations: (702) 740-6969; (866) 606-7111
Show Times: Tues.–Wed. and Fri.–Sun. 7:30 p.m. and 10:30 p.m.,
dark Mon. and Thurs.
Minimum Age: 18
Ticket Price: $81.90/$92.90/$114.90; sofa seating, 2/$293.30
Seating: Assigned seating
Beverage Service: Yes
Website: zumanity.com

SPW: 45%

If you go to zumanityhoops.com, you'll find a "game" you can play online called "Zumanity Hoops," in which you get to try to undress the delectable Julia Kolosova. Julia starts out wearing a sexy schoolgirl outfit—a plaid miniskirt, over-the-knee white stockings, and a top that looks more like a bra than a blouse. While Julia adopts sexy poses and spins multiple chrome hula hoops, you can undress her by following a gold ball with your cursor. Try to keep your eyes on that damn ball while Julia's spreading her legs in those little white panties. If you can actually get Julia's bra off, you're a better man than I am! Then again, play this game for a few minutes and tell me you don't want to see Julia do this act live while dangling from the ceiling on ropes!

For my money, the breathtaking gymnast/aerialist Julia Kolosova is the highlight of Cirque du Soleil's *Zumanity*.

But any strip-club devotee will find a half-dozen performances that make this production well worth the price of admission. The beautiful dancer/gymnast, Gyula Karaeva, who performs topless with her male partner in an oversized water bowl, is also incredibly sexy. Another aerialist, Robyn Houpt, does a heart-stopping bondage routine while hanging from the ceiling on black straps. All of these gifted athletes have such gorgeous bodies that they'll leave you spellbound. There are also several sexy male-female ballet-type dances with varying themes, including a bathtub number with gymnast Vanessa Convery and a male-female "hand-balancing" act. Frankly, if you like watching gorgeous naked women, you'd be making a big mistake if you passed on this show. The price is high, but it's definitely one-of-a-kind.

Surprise! It's Funny!

I was surprised at how funny the show is. My previous experience with Cirque du Soleil shows is limited to *Mystère* and *O*, neither of which would be labeled comedies in anybody's book. This show also has a cabaret feel to it, as a result of the live band, singers, and the comic performers who appear throughout.

The MC is a drag queen, à la Frank-N-Furter in the *Rocky Horror Picture Show*, though the comedy duo of Nicky Dewhurst and Shannon Calcutt, who specialize in audience-participation humor with a lot of improv, spend much more time on stage bantering with the crowd. They're very funny. Dewhurst is a skinny guy in a bad-fitting powder-blue suit with a sleazy leer. Calcutt is scrawny and goofy-looking in an outfit reminiscent of a 1950s' high-school-prom dress with lots of petticoats. She has a voice that could cut glass. Her bit on how flat girls can improvise a boob job with scotch-filled baggies is truly demented.

Then there are the Botero Sisters, identical twins who are quite a few pounds beyond zaftig. Think hippos in tutus. Appearing first dressed as sexy French maids and subsequently in various skimpy lingerie ensembles, these

Snyder Says: More than one bizarre moment, but you can't help but laugh.

girls are downright fat and proud of it. If you have the nerve to sit up front, you may find one of them in your lap or smothering you in her titties (hey—the only casino show in Vegas with lap dancing!), or simply feeding you strawberries from a silver tray. Later in the show they do a pom-pom dance with the aforementioned comedy duo, in which all appear to be naked while sporting fake genitals. Believe me, *Zumanity* has more than one bizarre moment, but it's all so silly you can't help but laugh out loud.

The Zumanity Theatre is large (seating 1,256), with a big stage that juts into the center of the high-ceilinged room. It's an excellent design for this show; there really aren't any bad seats. Even the balcony seats are steeply tiered so that everyone has a good view of the stage. The front-row seats are comfy sofas for two and can only be purchased in pairs ($293.30 per loveseat). Even though you'll pay extra for one of these, this is definitely a show that you'd like an up-front seat for, but don't sit up front if you don't want to risk being a part of the production. Even if you're not right up front, cast members go through the audience at times picking victims for various weird comedy skits.

No drinks are served in the theater, but you can bring one in with you. Full bars in both the lobby and

The scrumptious Julia Kolosova of *Zumanity*

balcony serve domestic beer for $6. It's a 90-minute show, so I'd suggest getting a drink or two.

Warning: You'll have to sit through a number of acts that may not be your cup of beer if it's really just the hot babes you're interested in, such as a male striptease number and a double-jointed male contortionist who comes out in boxer shorts and socks with old-fashioned sock-garters and proceeds to tie himself in knots. There's also a dance number where two men in a cage pantomime a fight that ends in them kissing passionately. Then there's the muscle-bound midget acrobat and the muscle-bound gigolo and the muscle-bound black dude with satyr's horns who walks on all fours.

But all in all, even if you just go for the babes, you won't be disappointed.

Index

Index

About the Author

Arnold Snyder is a professional gambler who lives in the mountains west of Las Vegas with his wife Karen, two dogs (Muddy and Mojo), four cats (Mookie, Titanic, Whitey, and Gabby), and a bunch of chickens who shall remain nameless. Since 1980, Arnold has written a dozen books on blackjack, poker, and Internet gambling. He was elected into the Blackjack Hall of Fame in 2003. He has lectured on the mathematics of gambling at major universities around the country and has appeared as an expert witness in numerous high-profile gambling-related court cases. When asked about his credentials as an expert on strip clubs, he simply points to his empty wallet. You may contact Arnold at: arnoldsnyder@live.com.

About Huntington Press

Huntington Press is a specialty publisher of
Las Vegas- and gambling-related books and
periodicals and the award-winning website
LasVegasAdvisor.com.

Huntington Press
3665 Procyon Street
Las Vegas, Nevada 89103
(702) 252-0655 • (800) 244-2224
HuntingtonPress.com